LETTER TRACING

A is for....

B is for....

Airplane

Bag

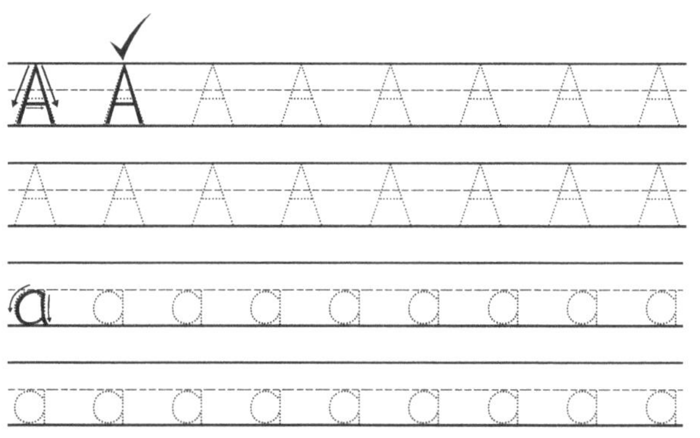

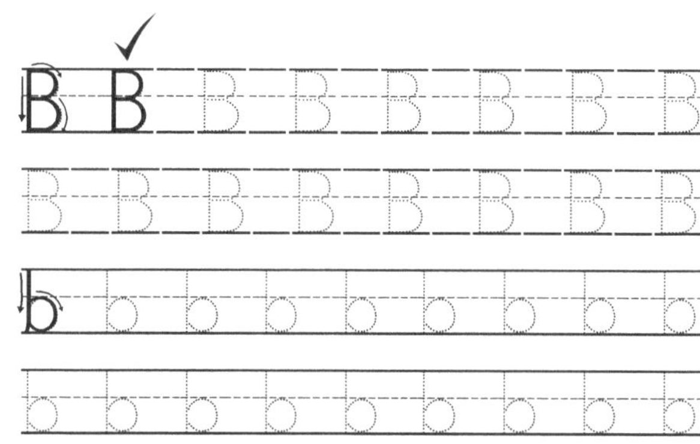

Follow the gray dots
to form the letters

A is for....

Airplane

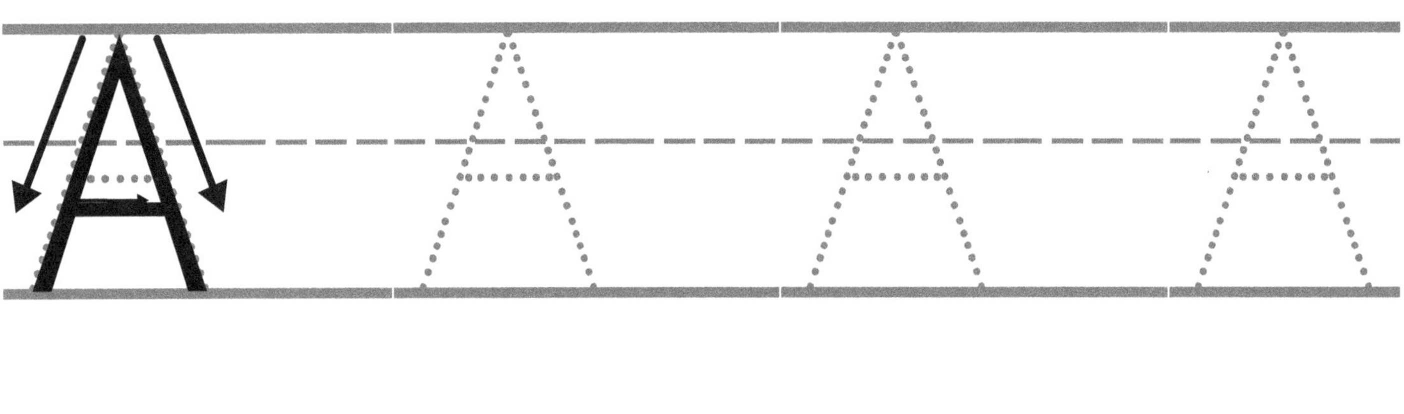

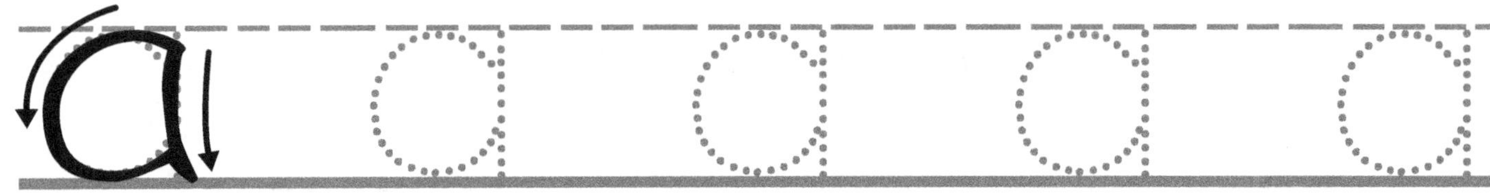

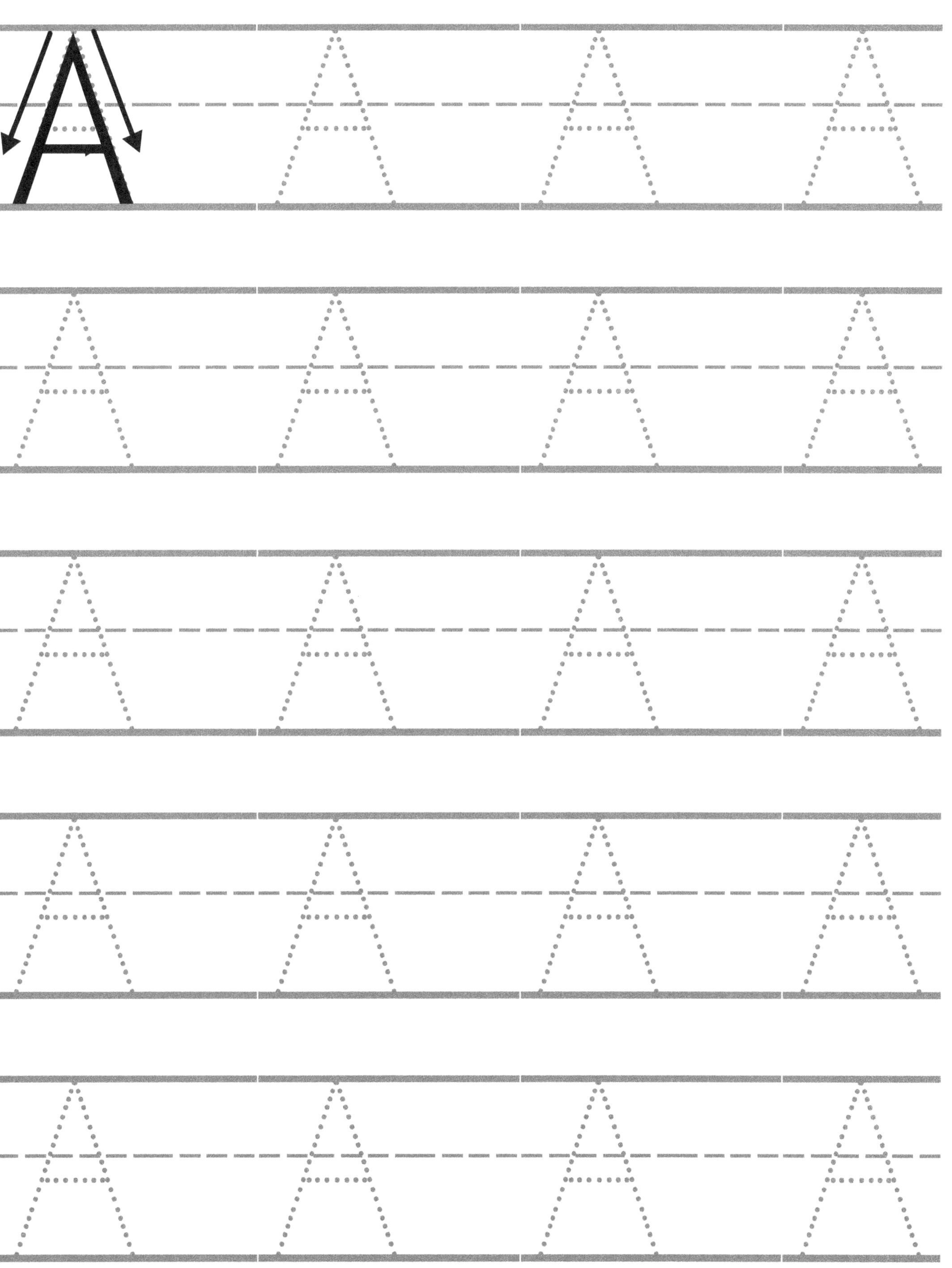

a a a a a

a a a a a

a a a a a

a a a a a

a a a a a

B is for....

Bag

B

b

C is for....

Cat

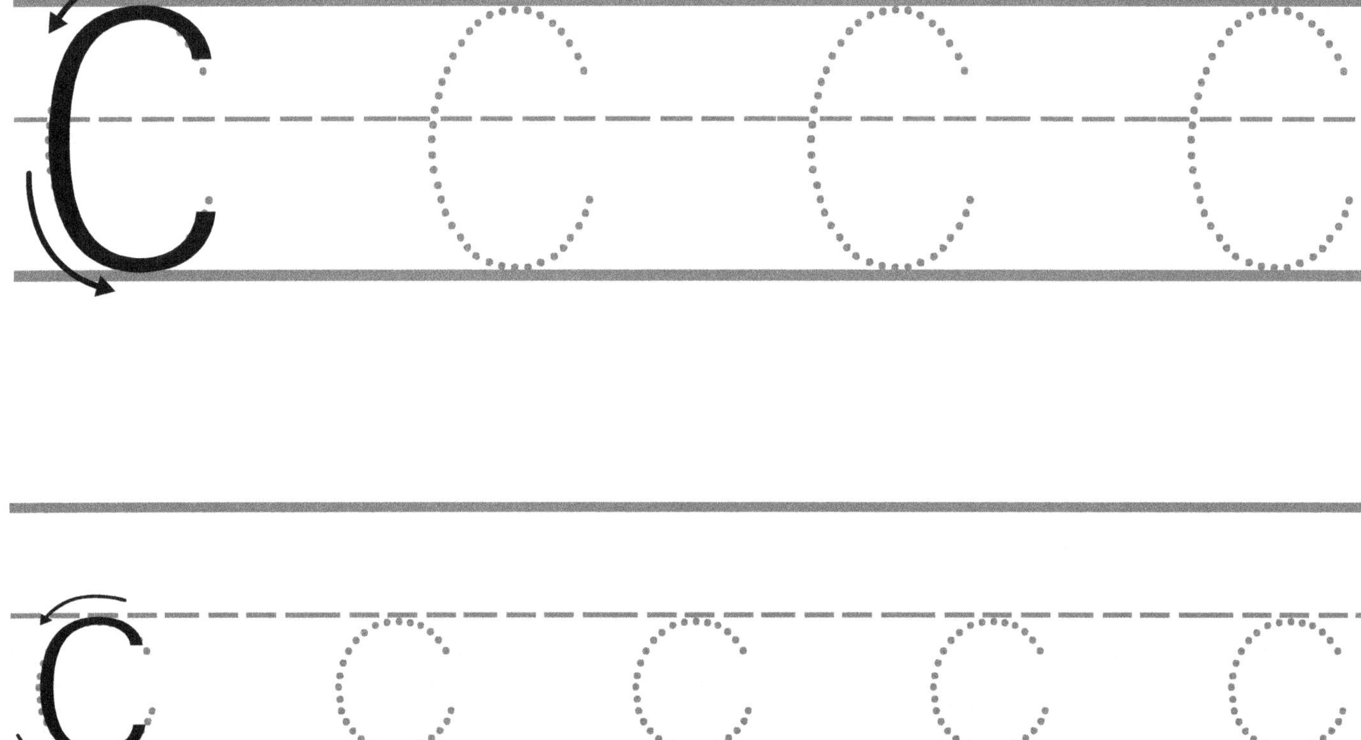

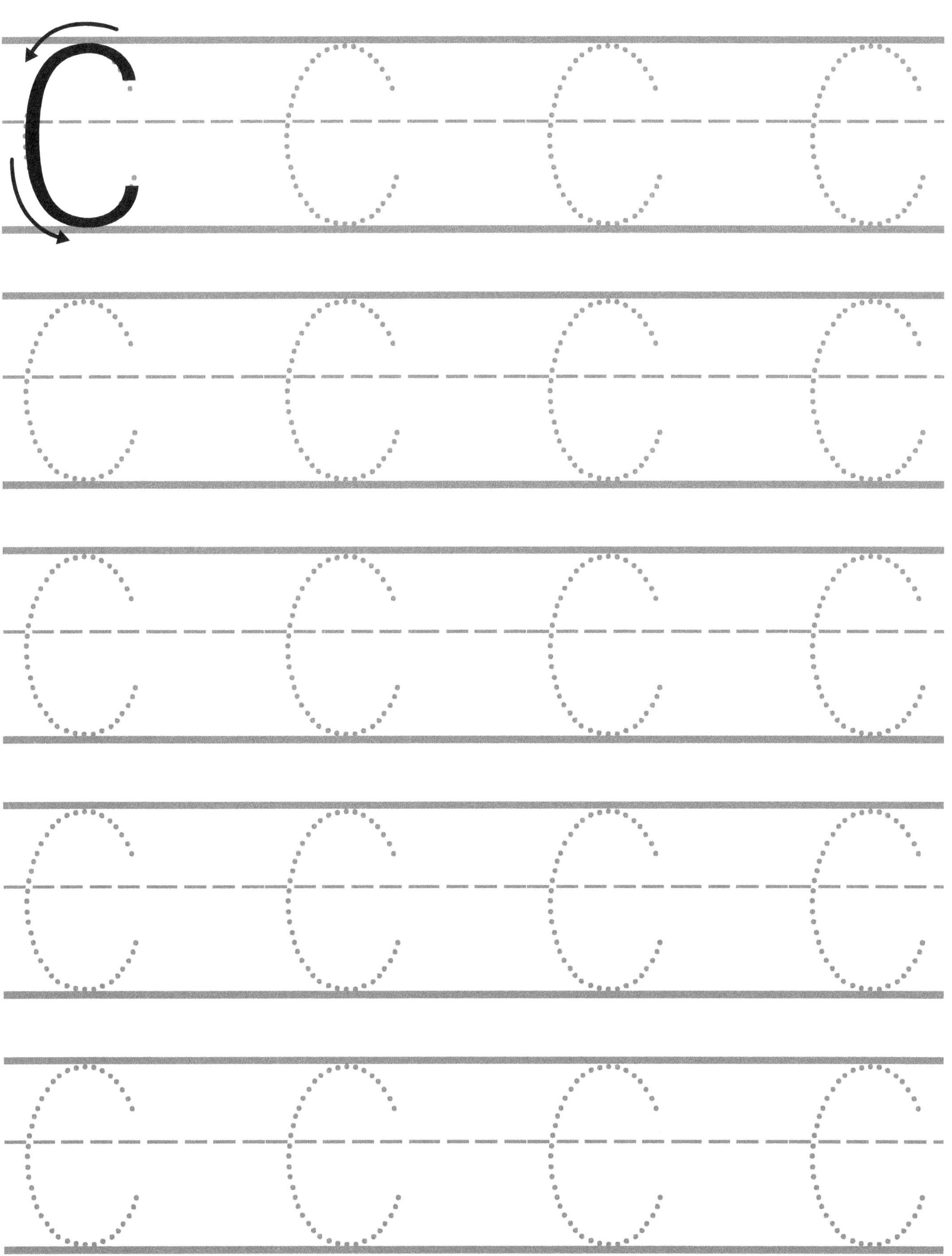

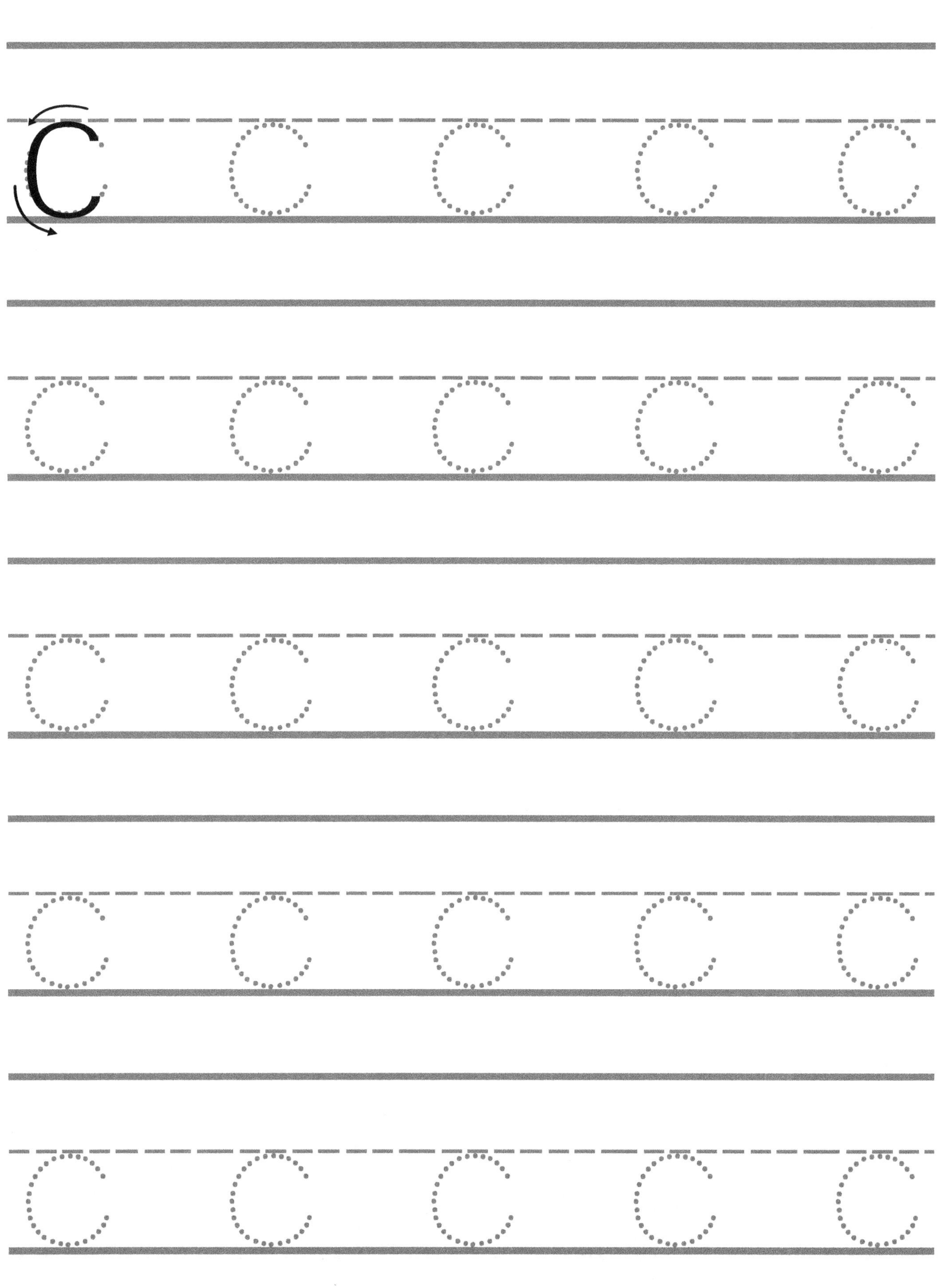

D is for....

Duck

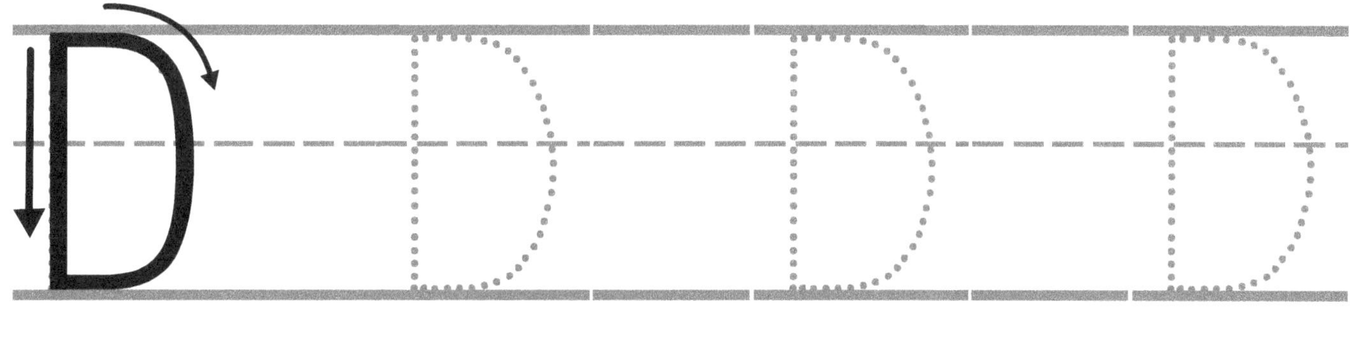

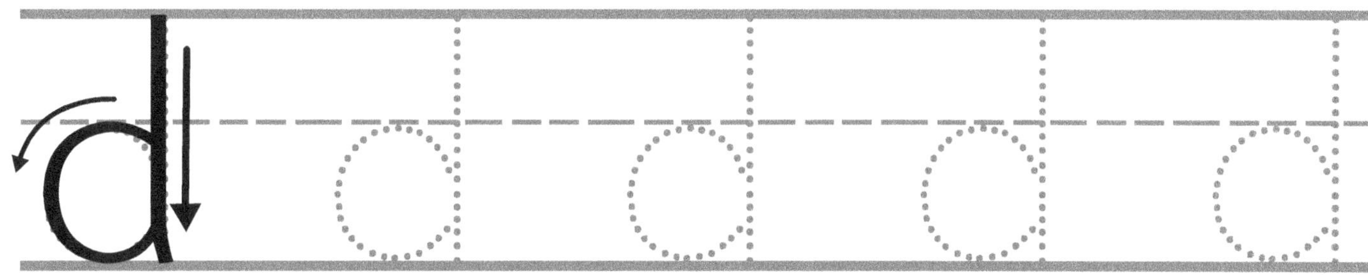

D

d

E is for....

Elephant

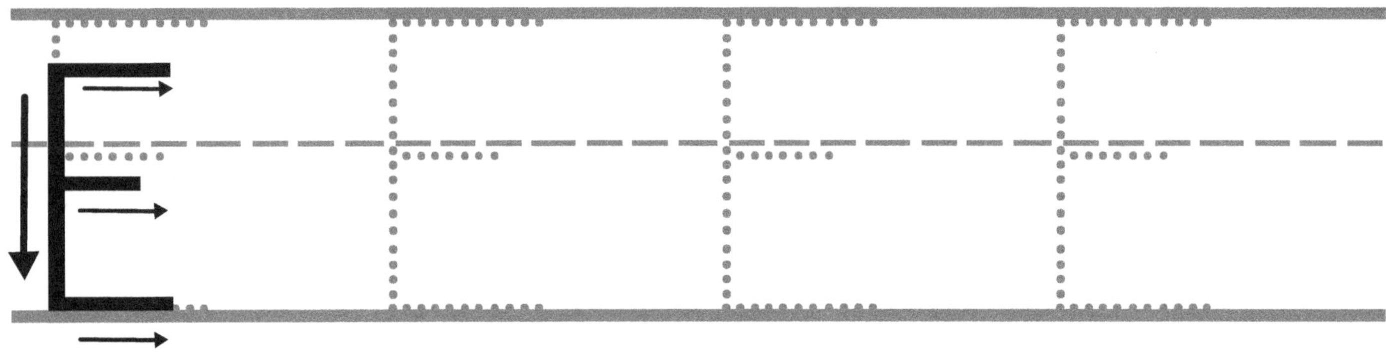

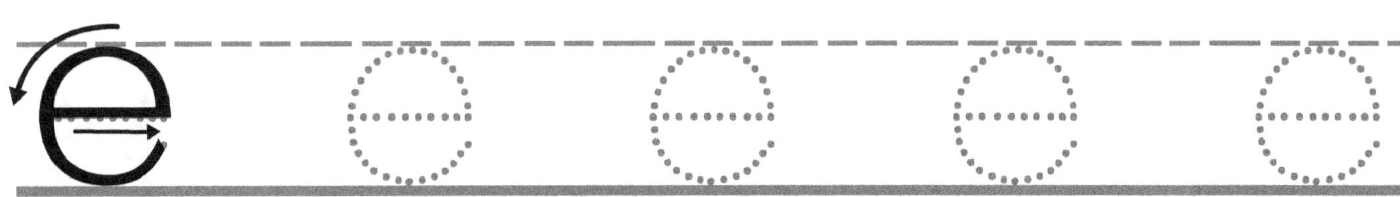

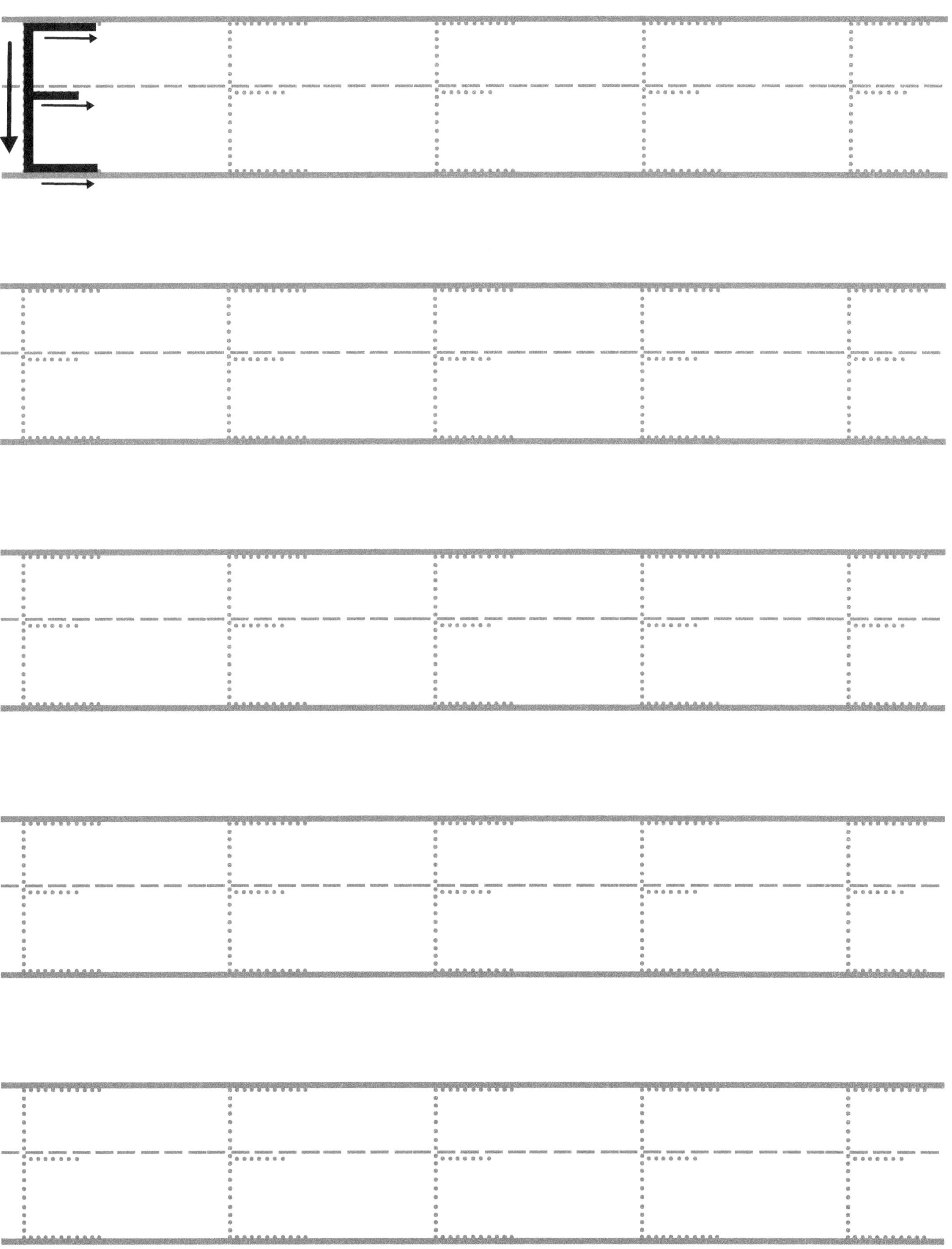

F is for....

Flamingo

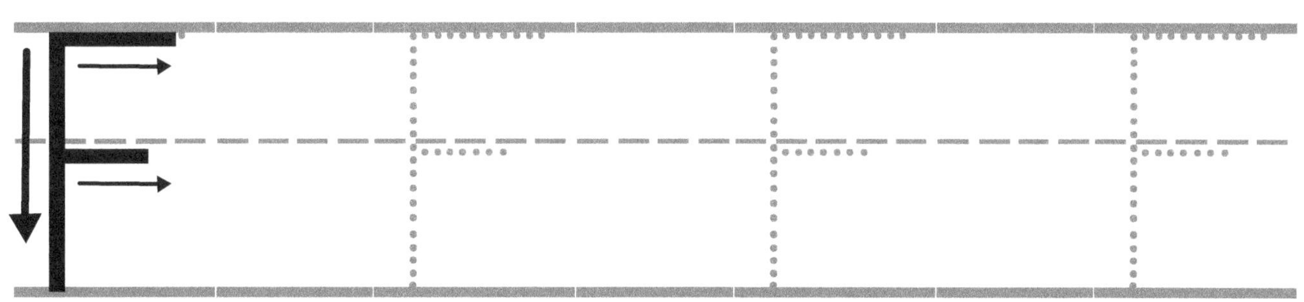

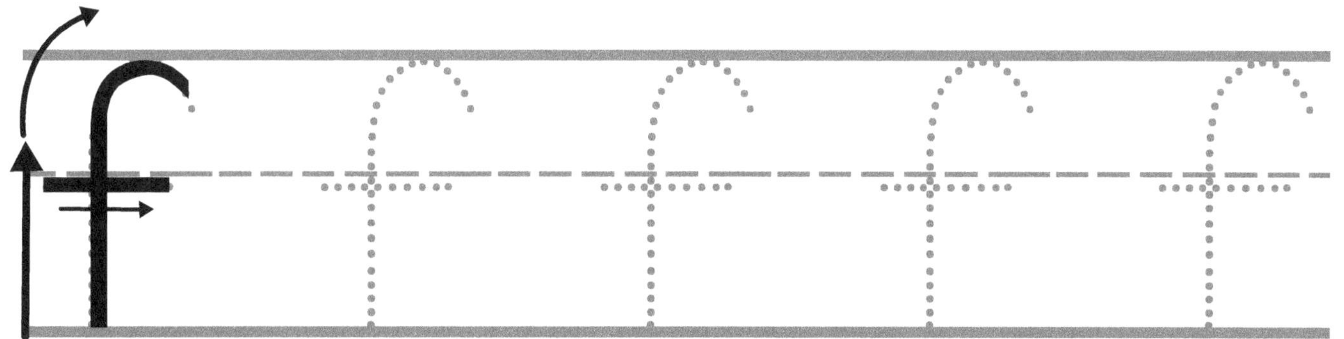

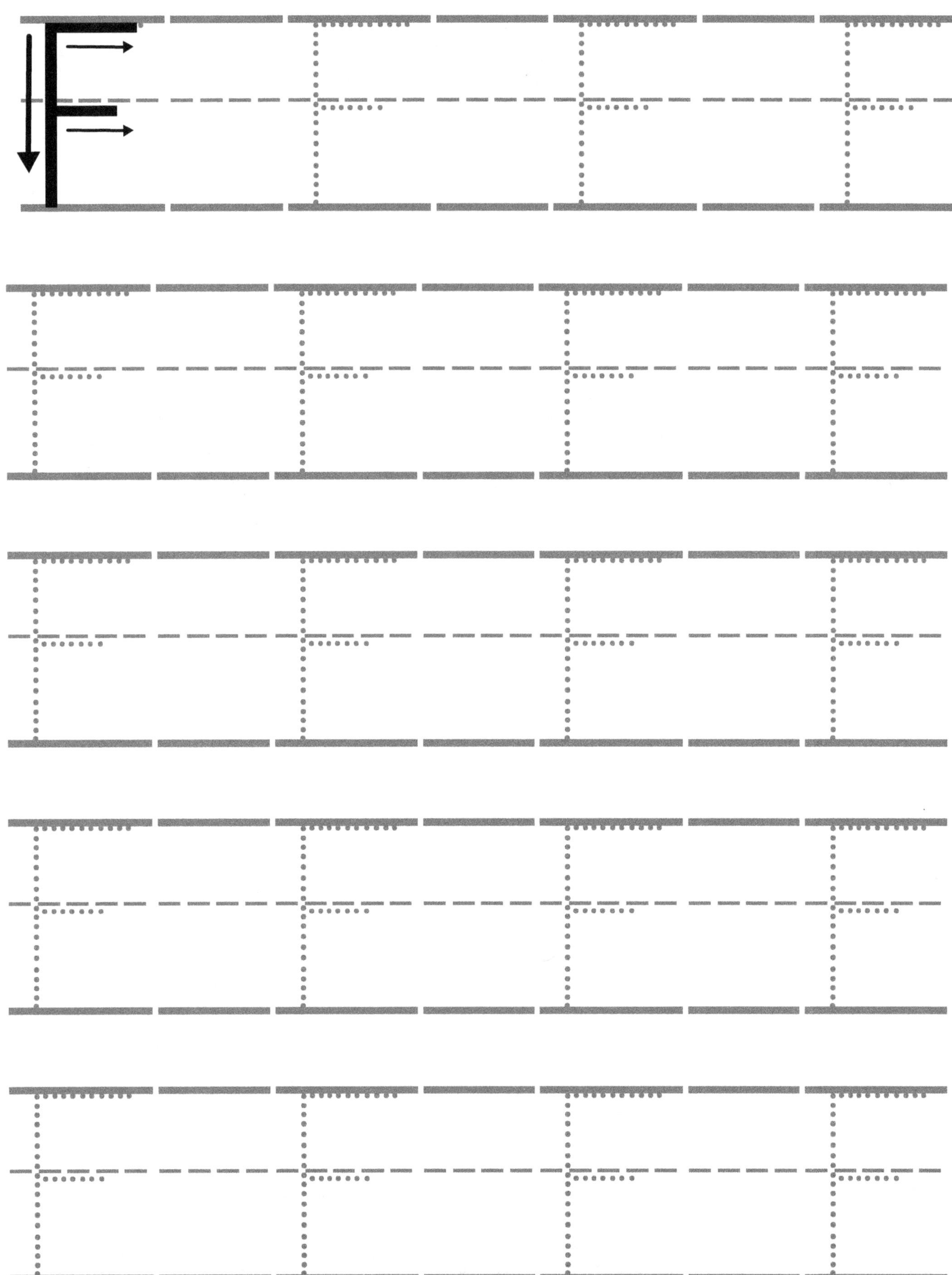

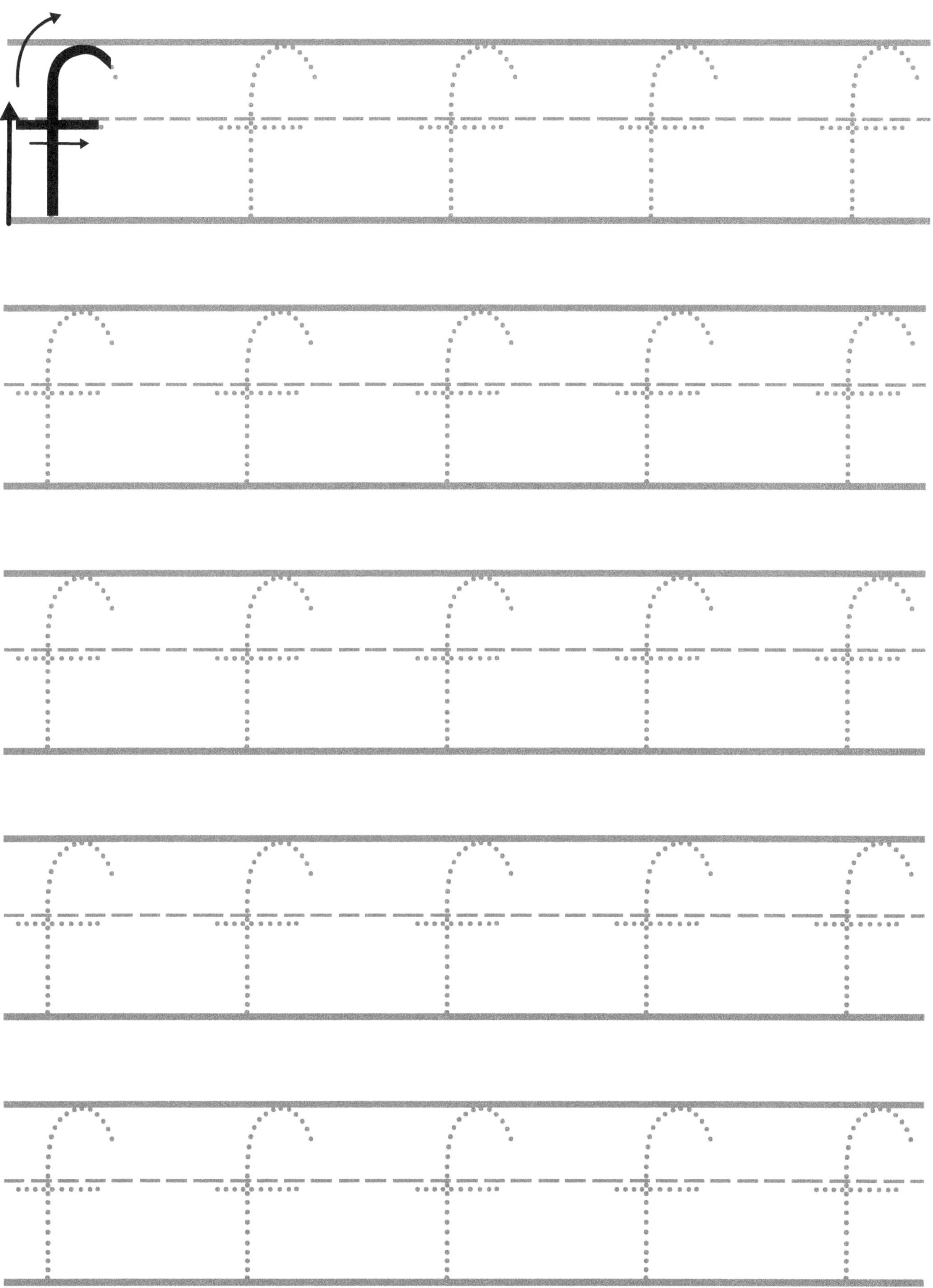

G is for....

Goose

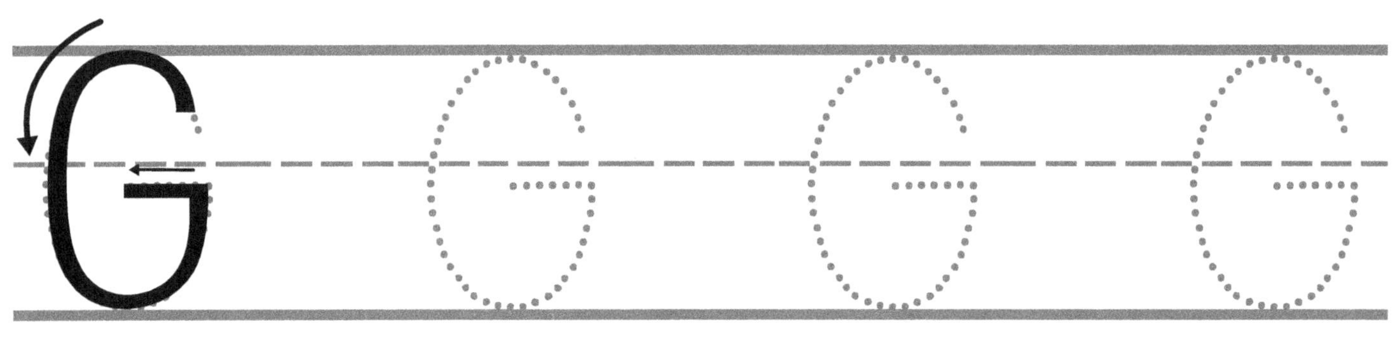

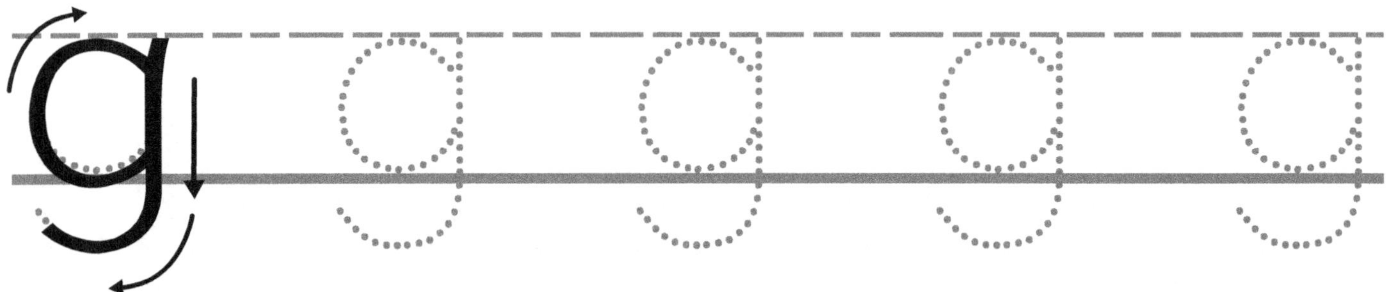

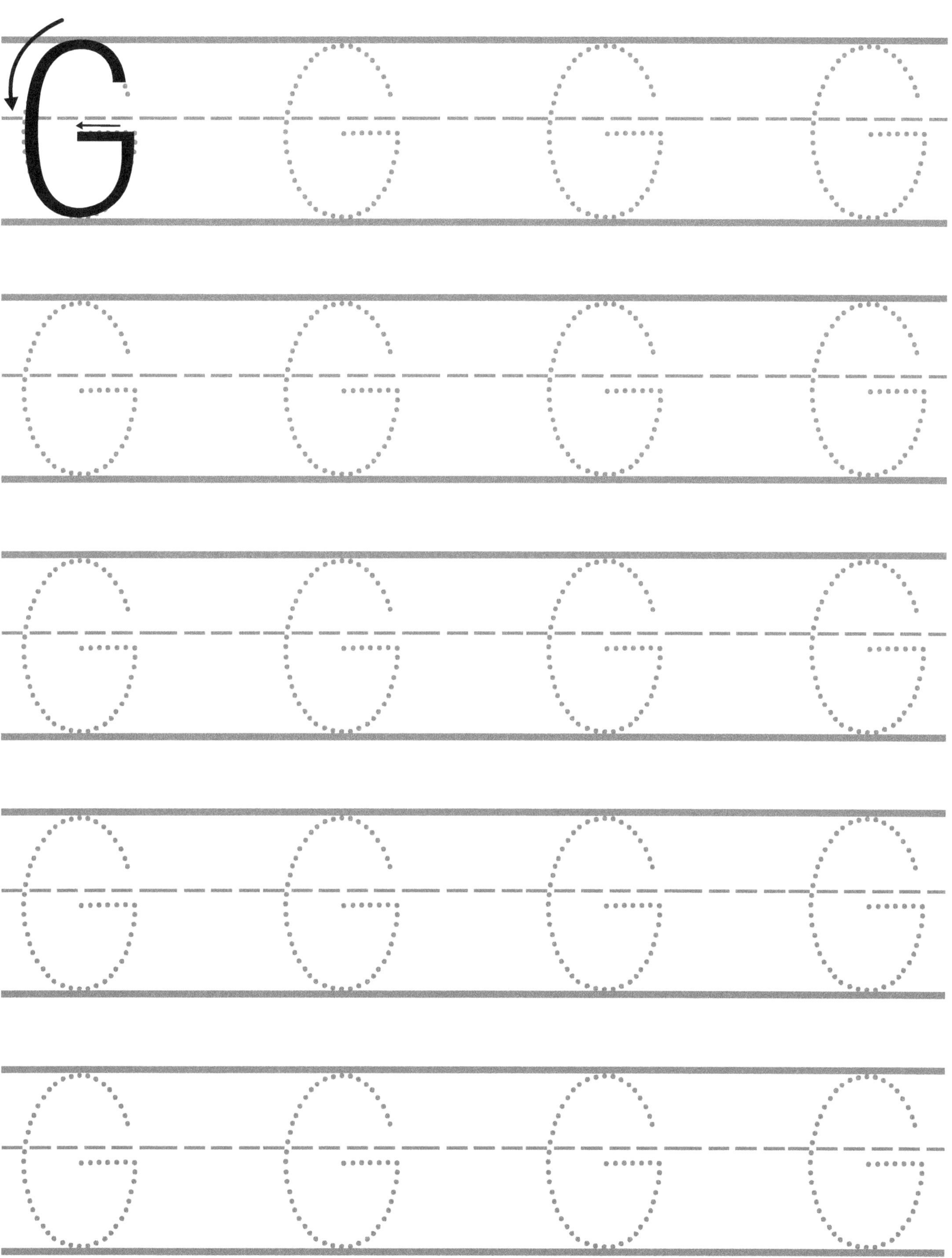

g

H is for....

Home

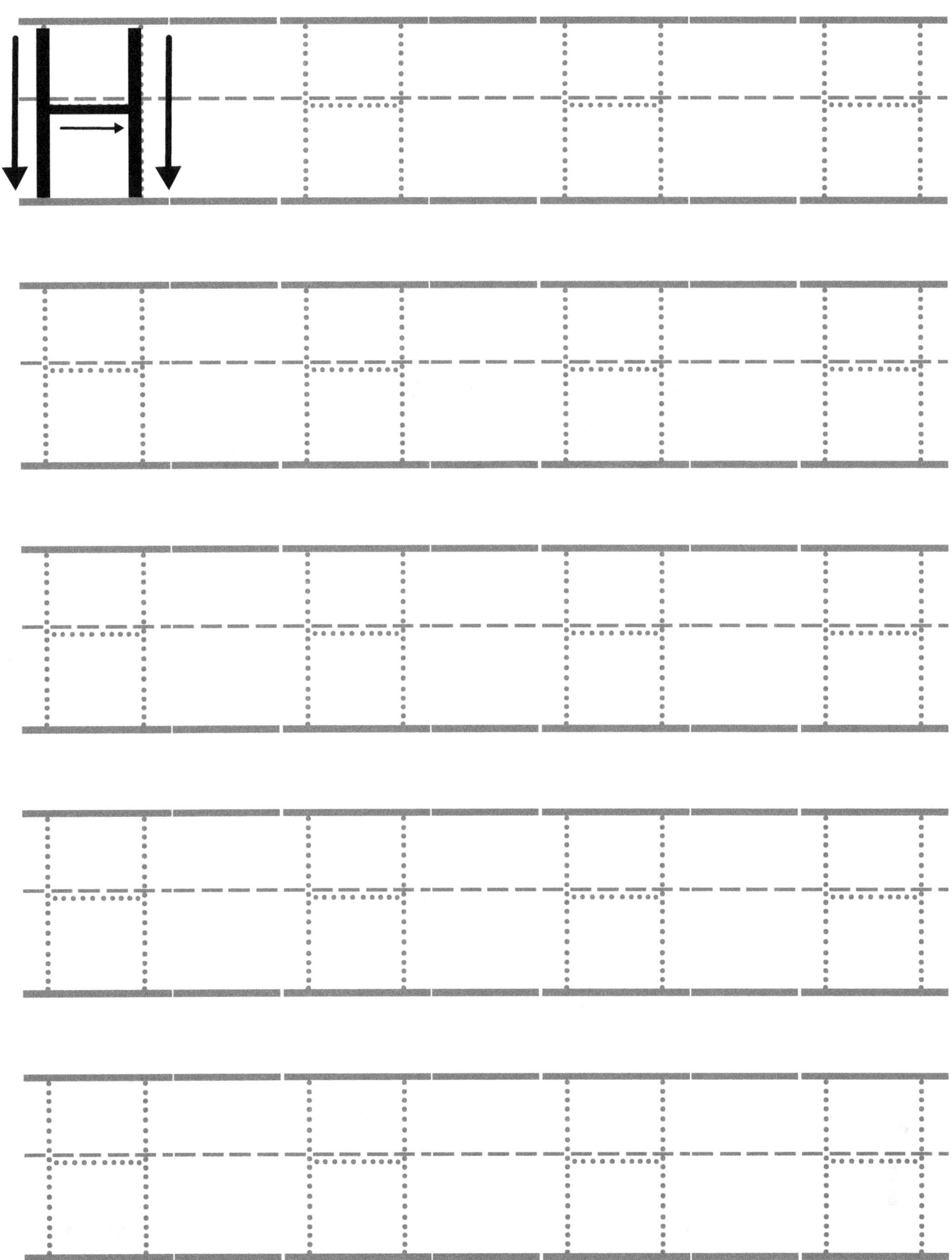

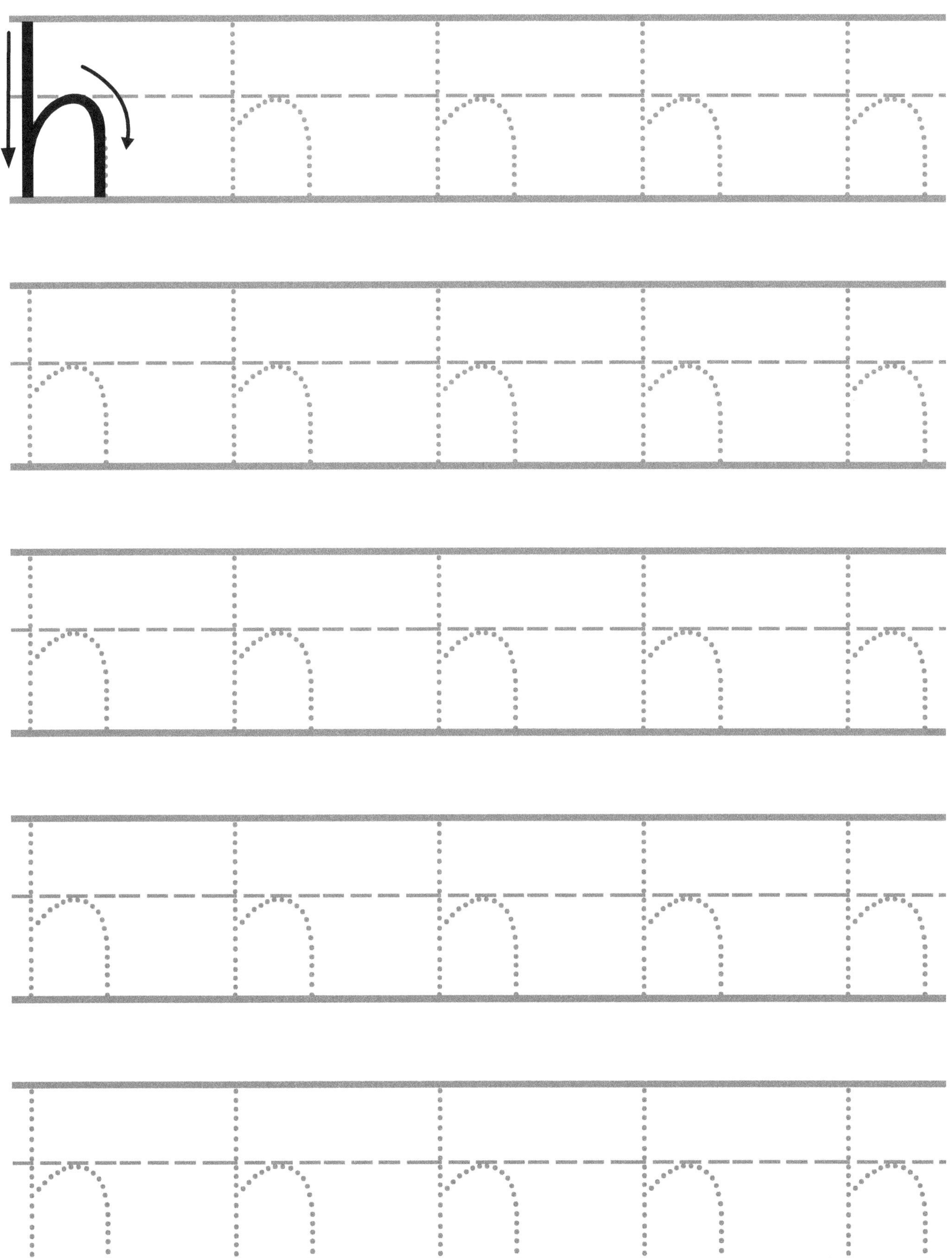

I is for....

Ice cream

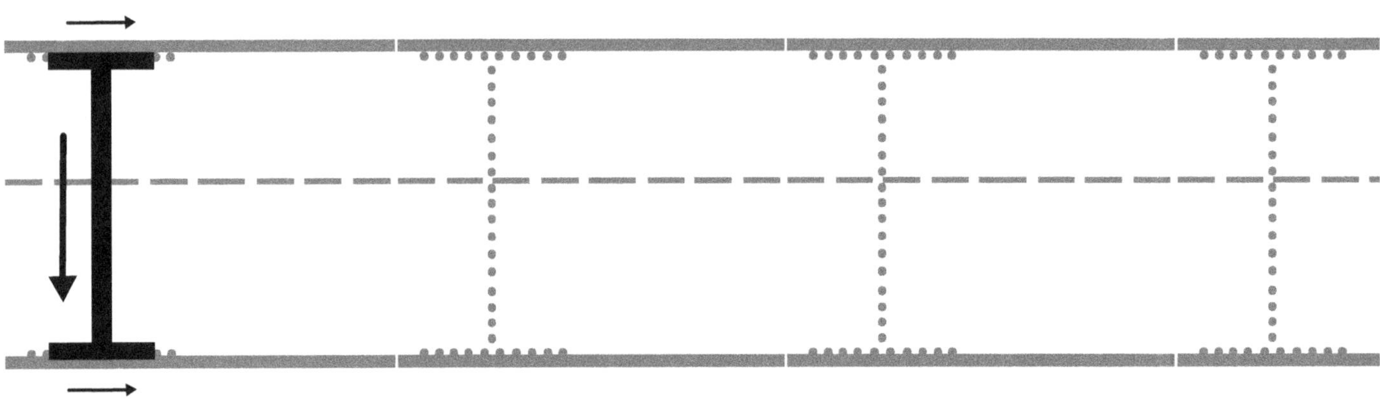

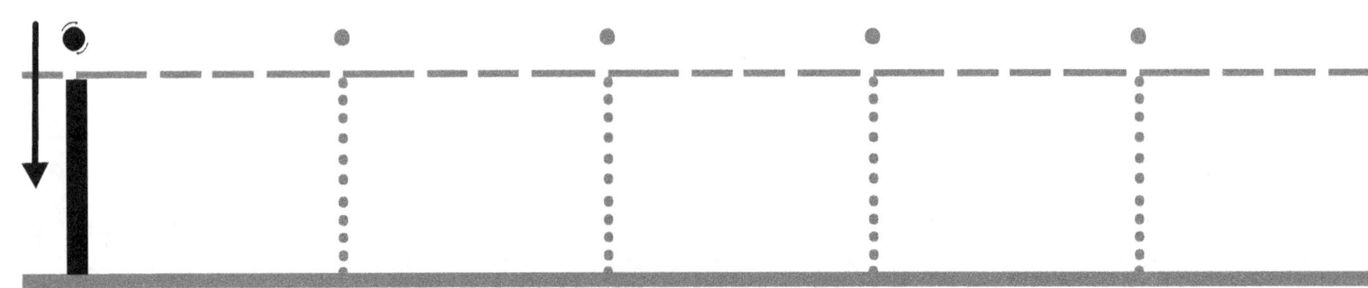

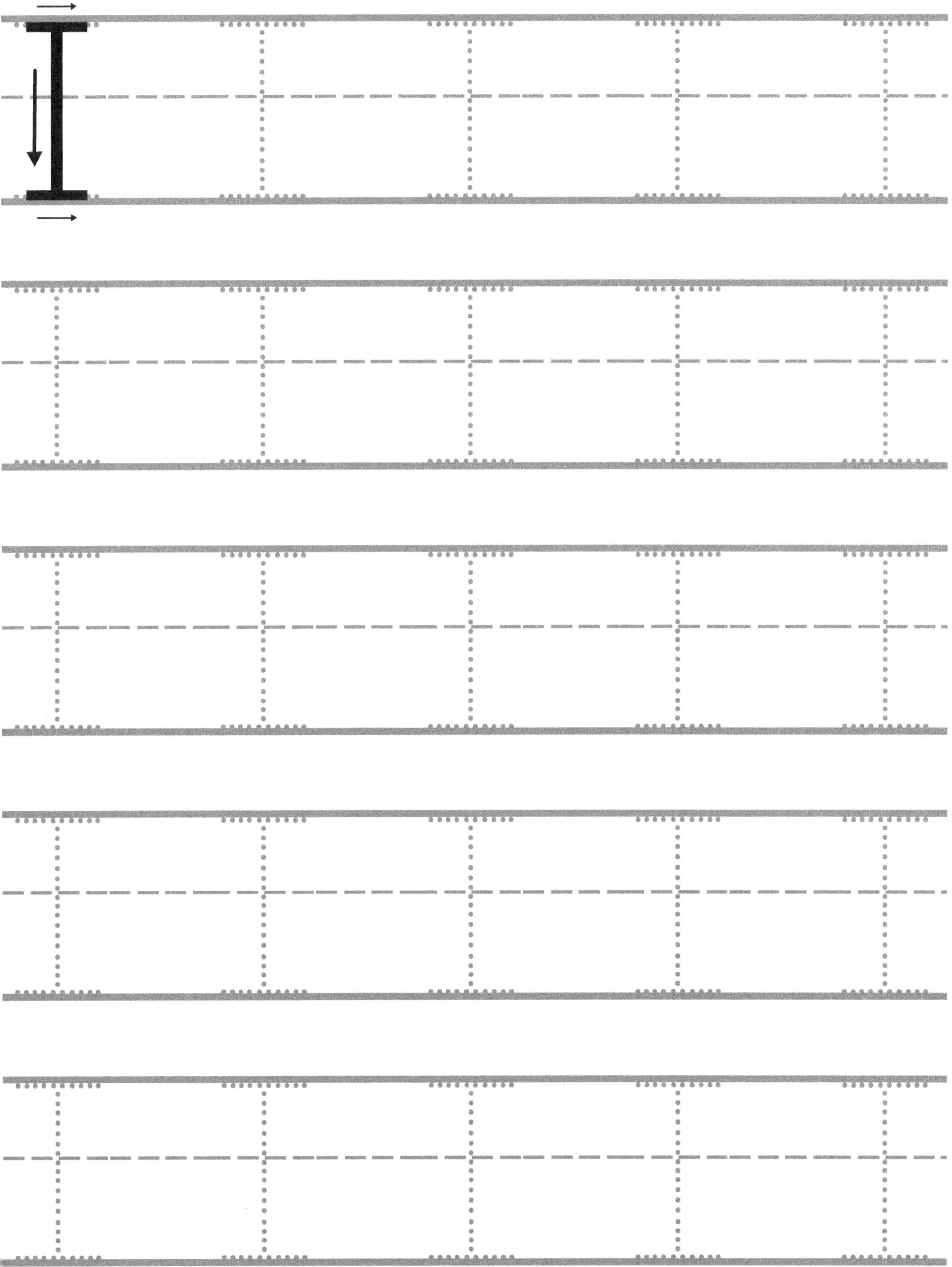

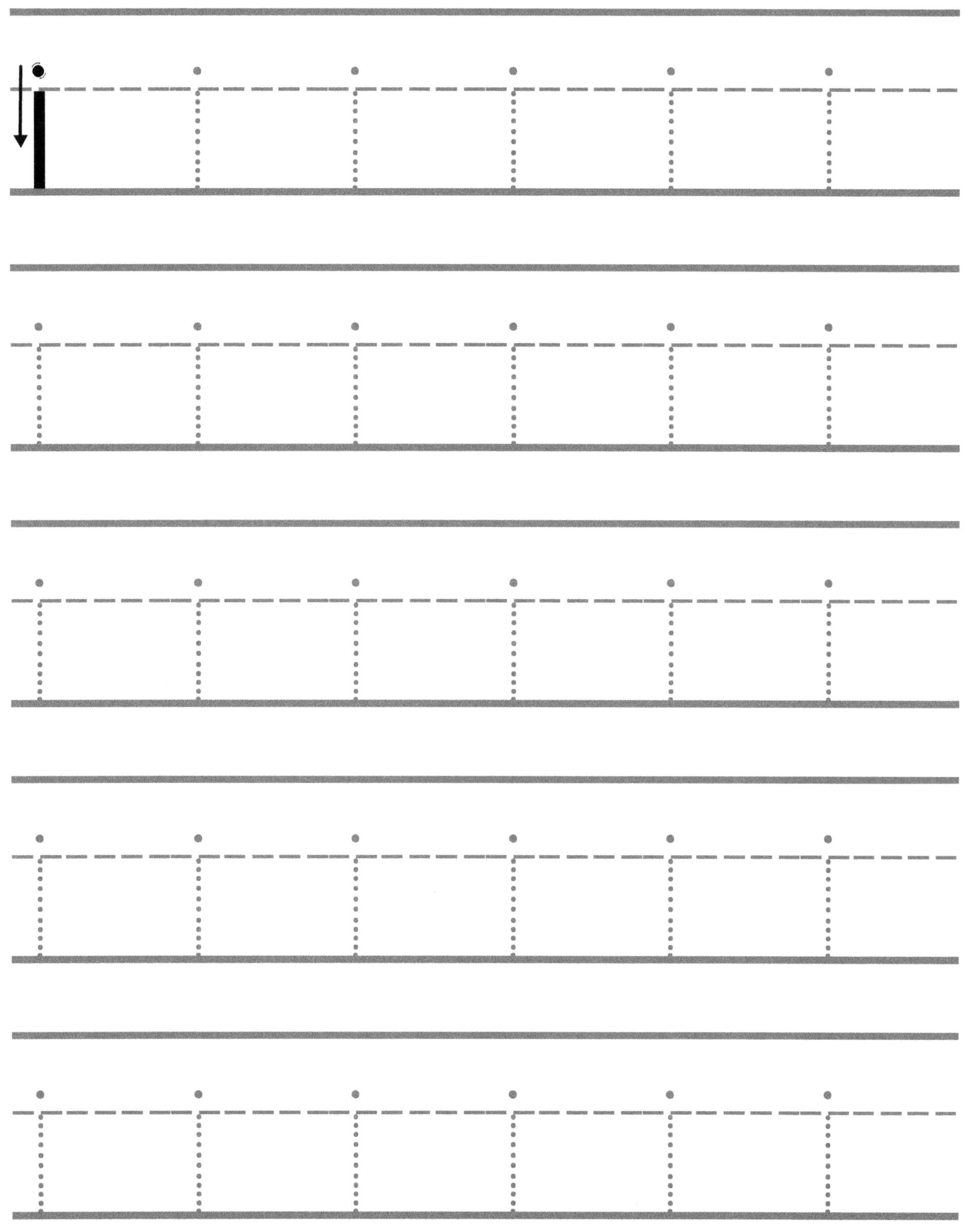

J is for....

Jellyfish

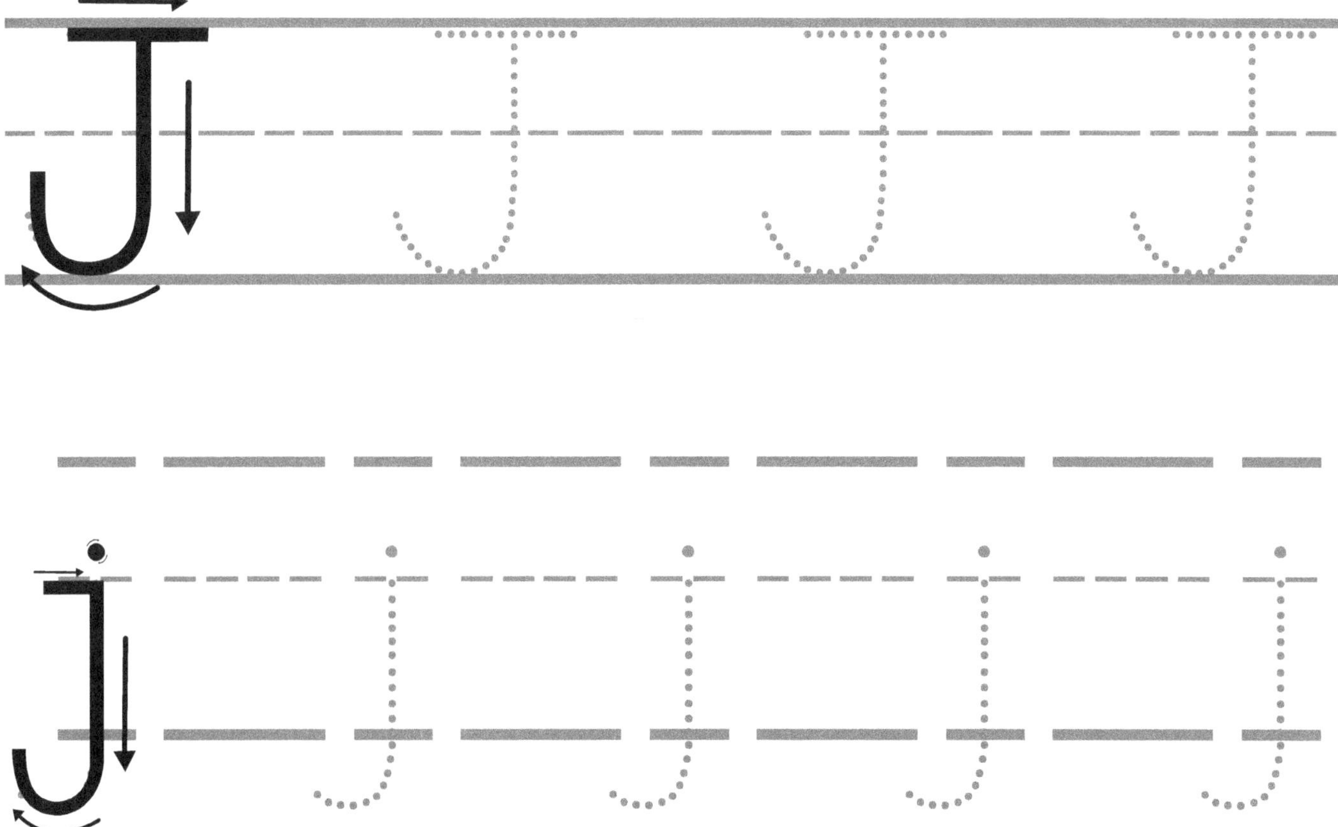

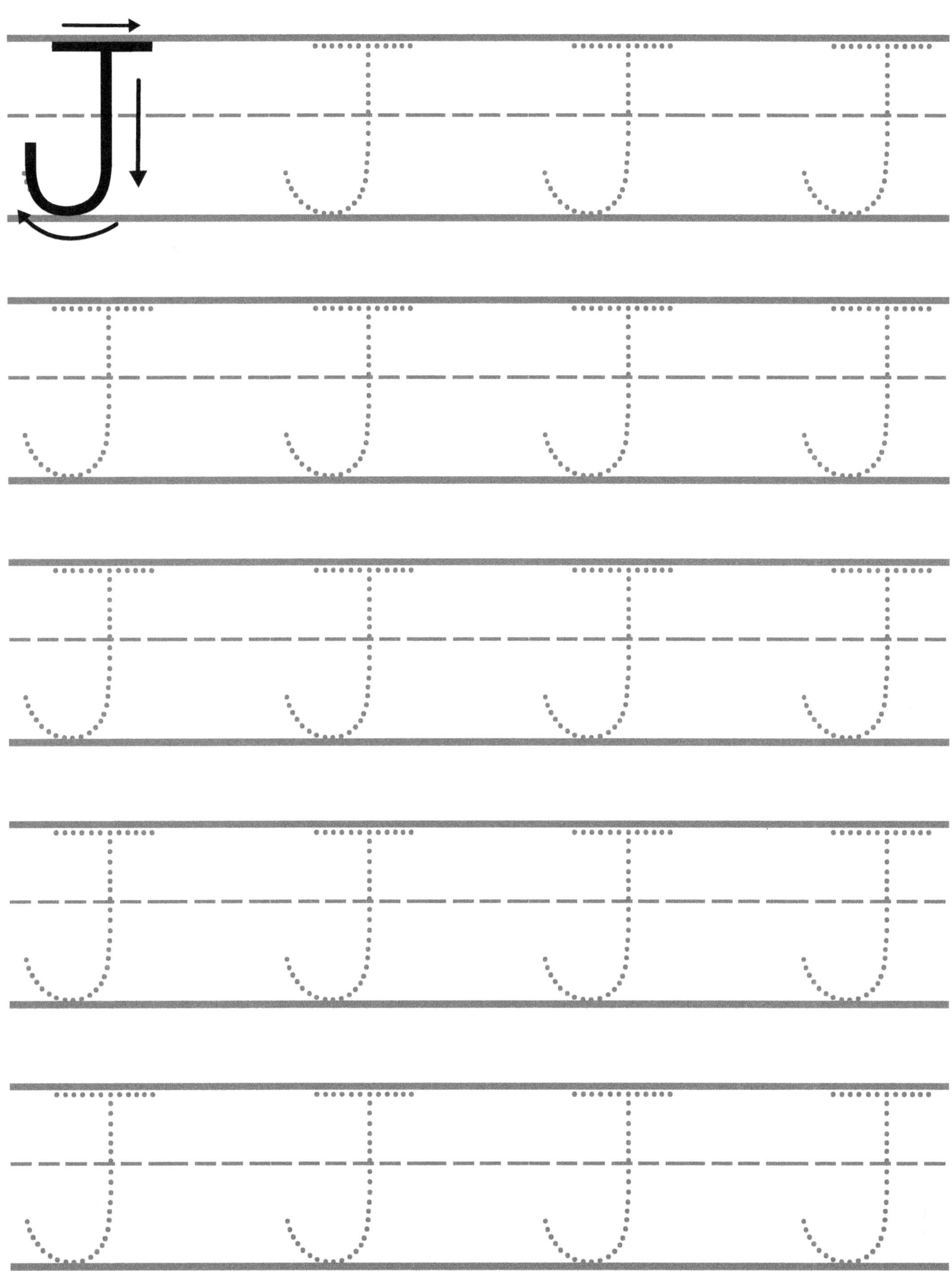

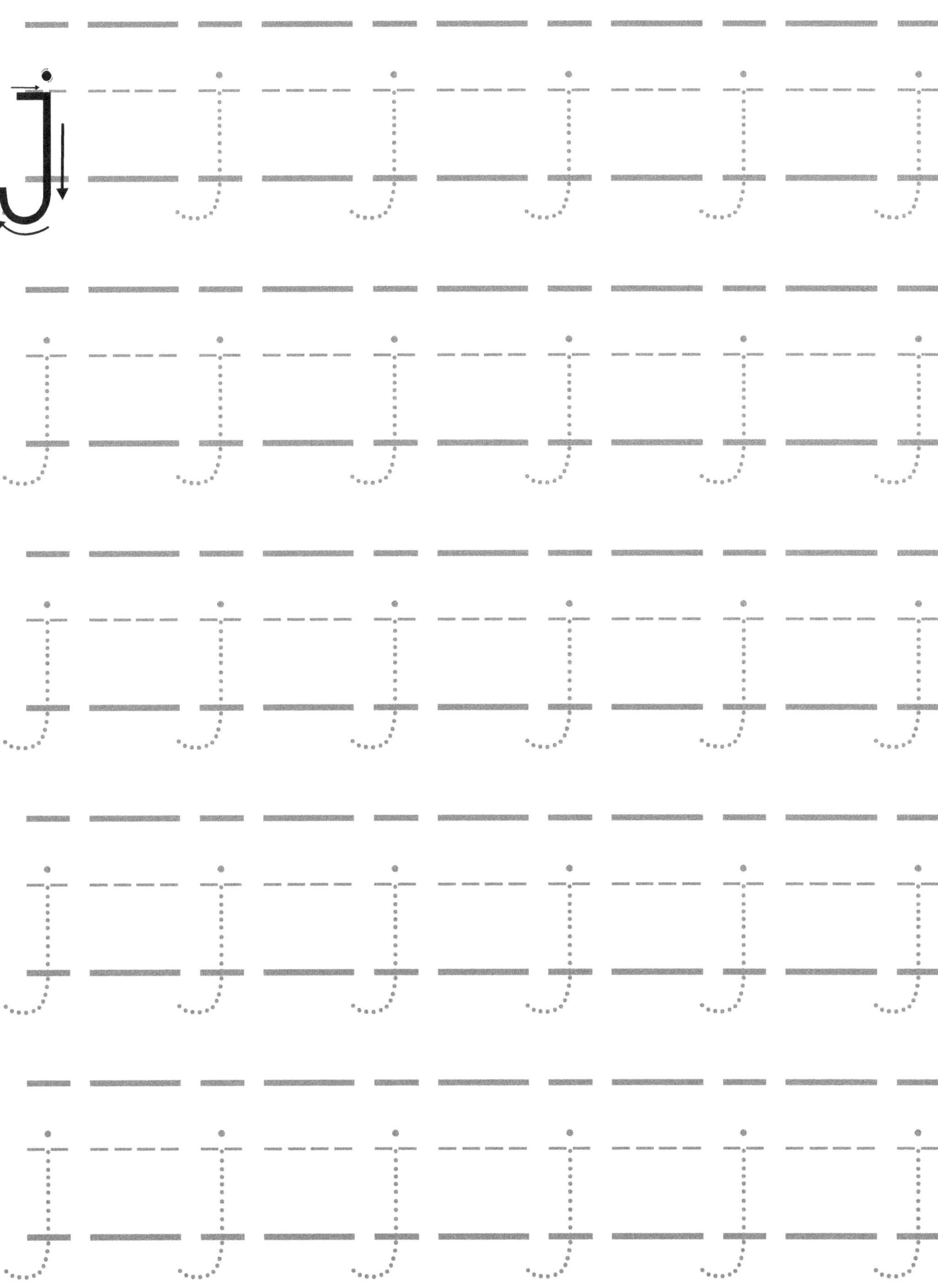

K is for....

Kangaroo

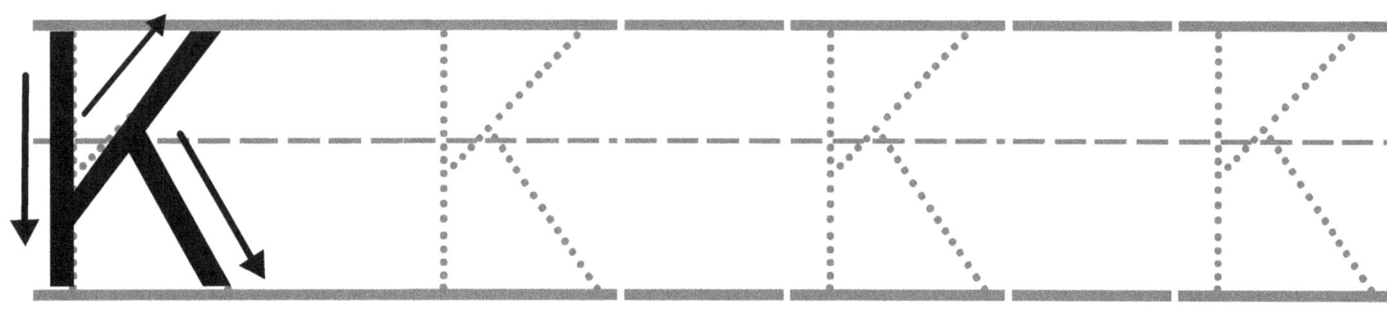

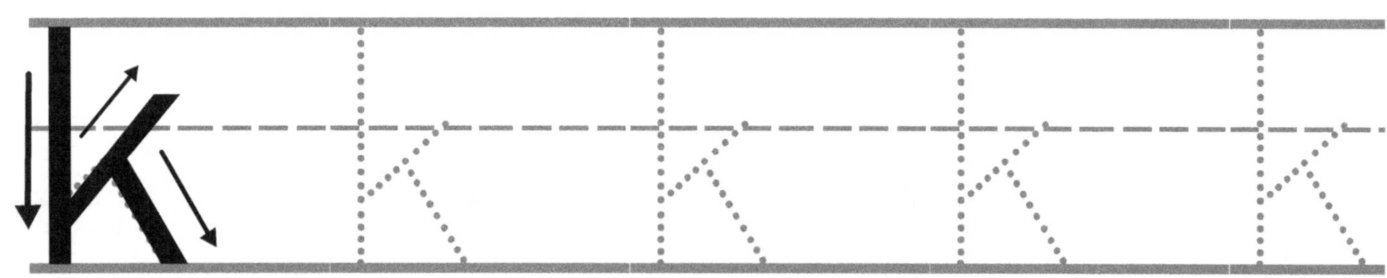

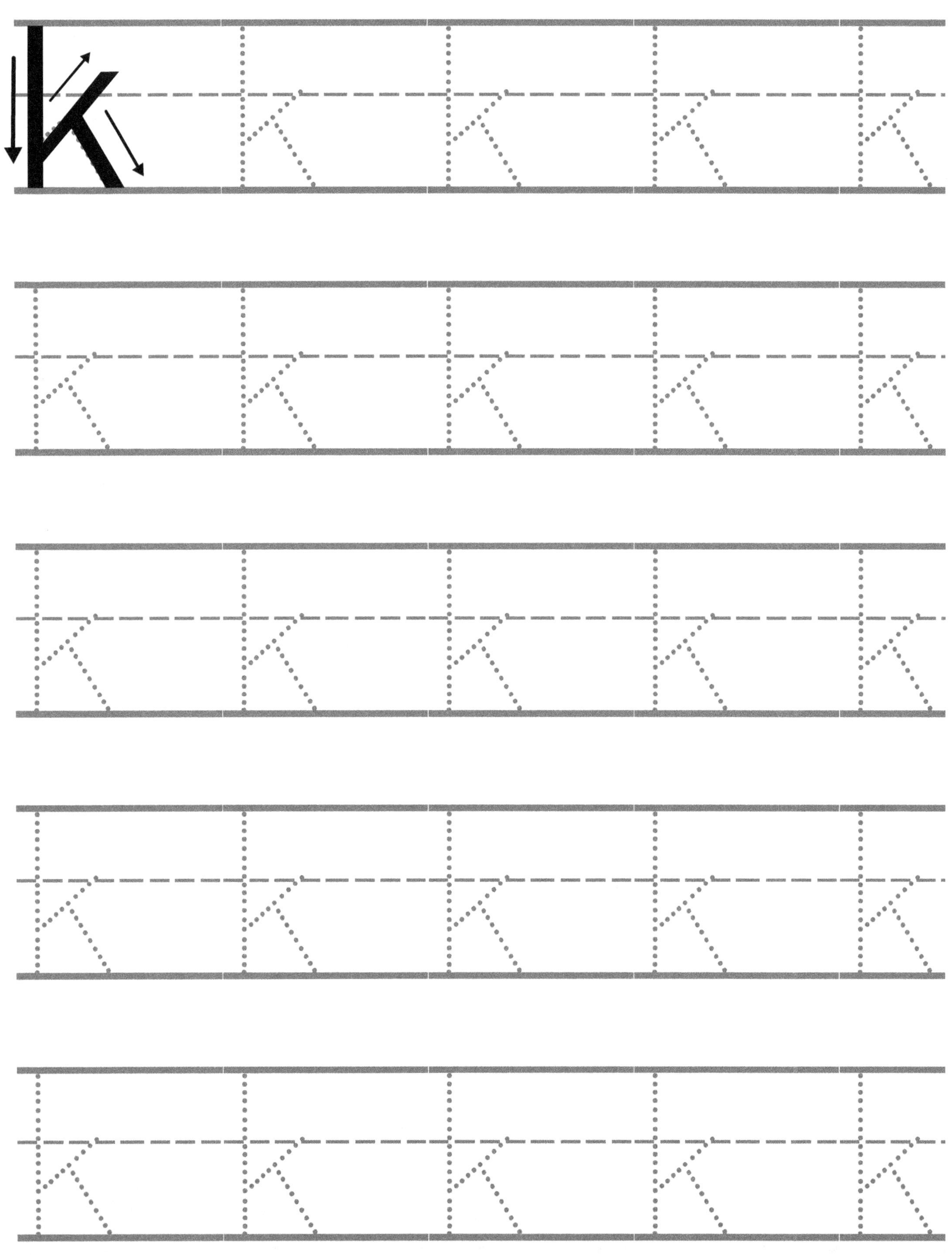

L is for....

Lamp

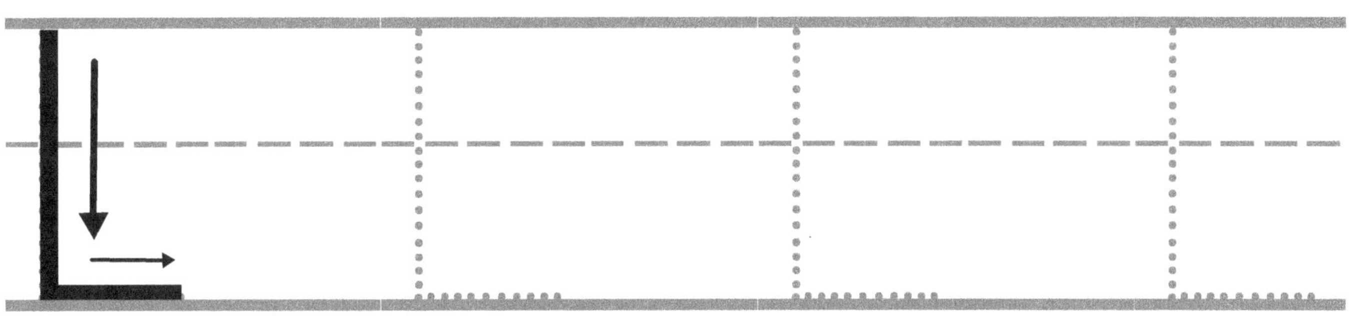

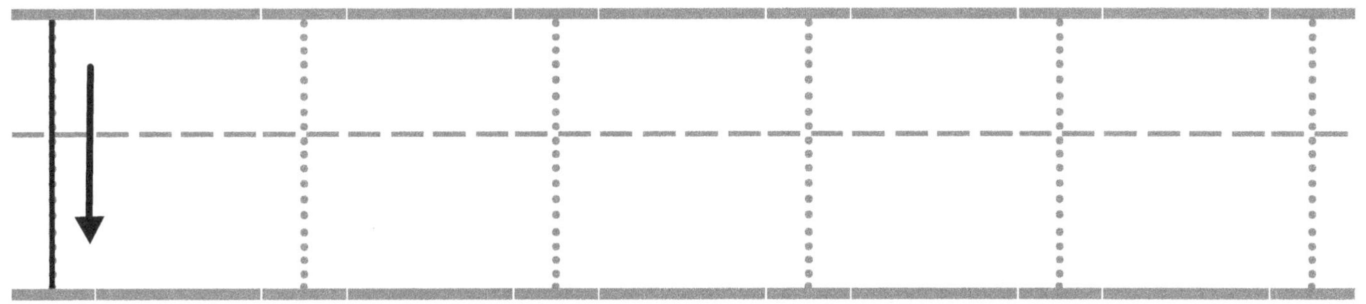

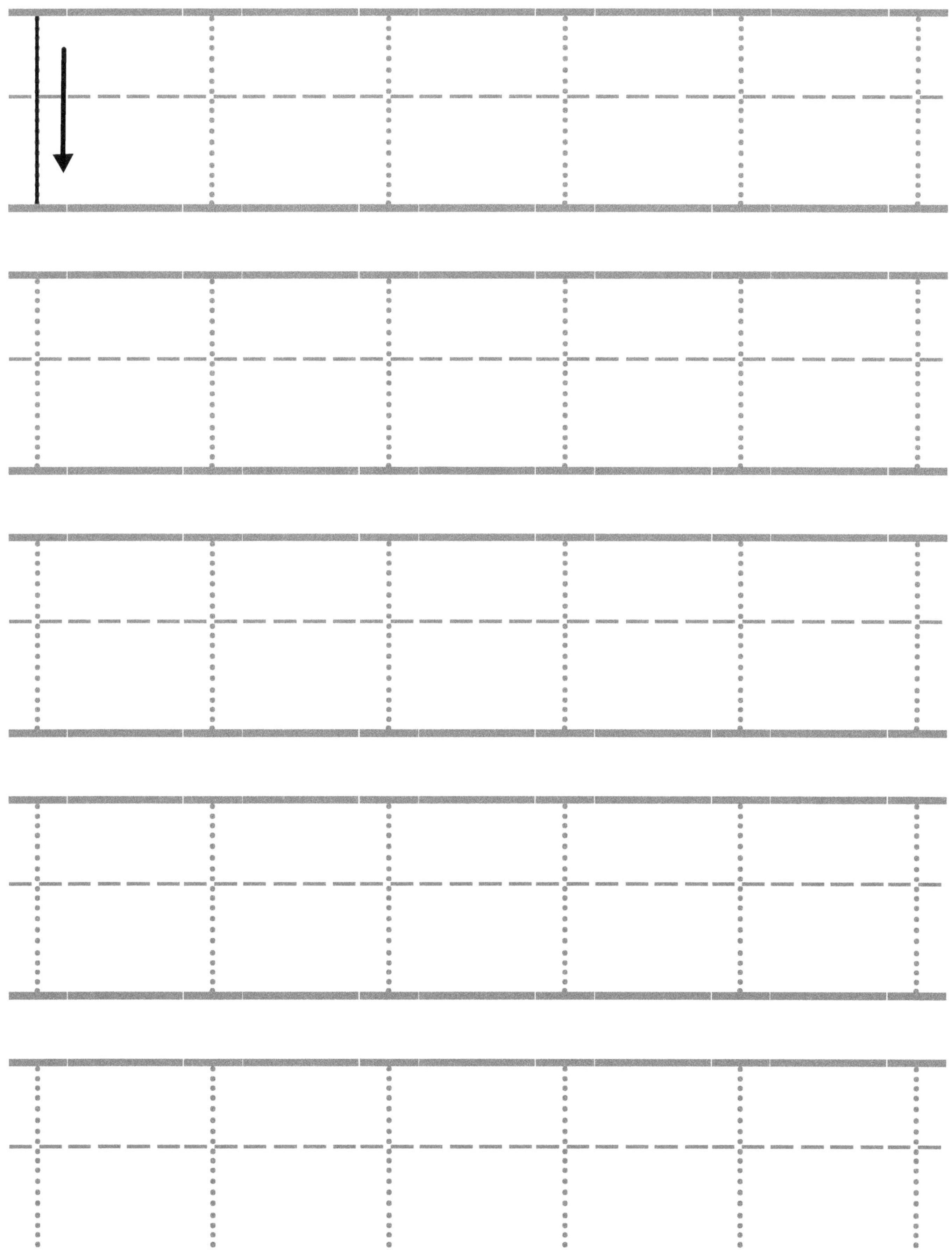

M is for....

Milk

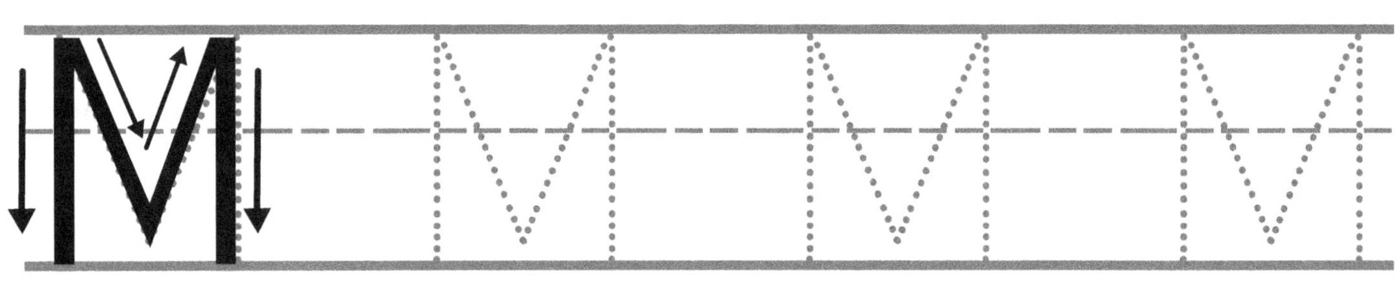

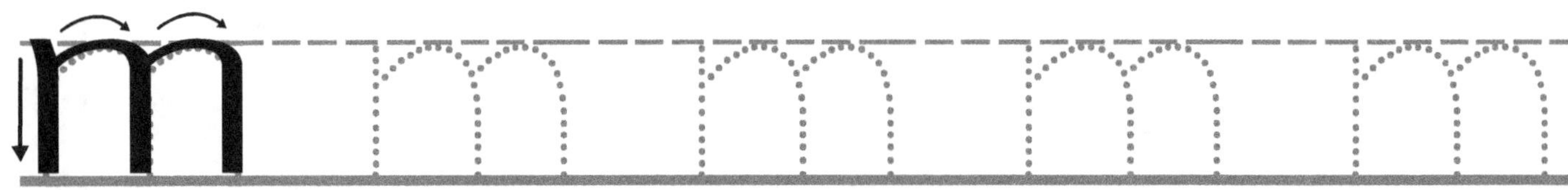

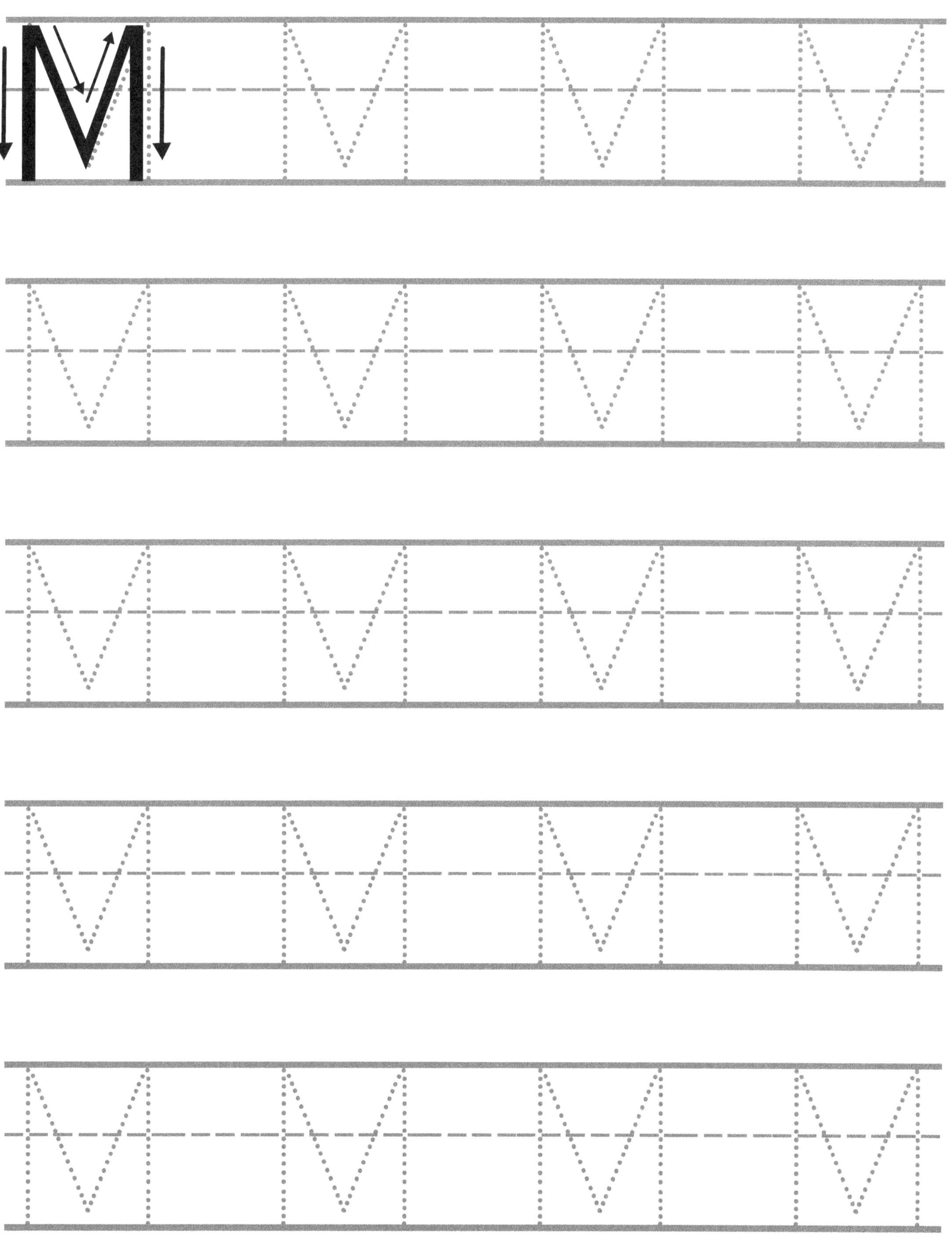

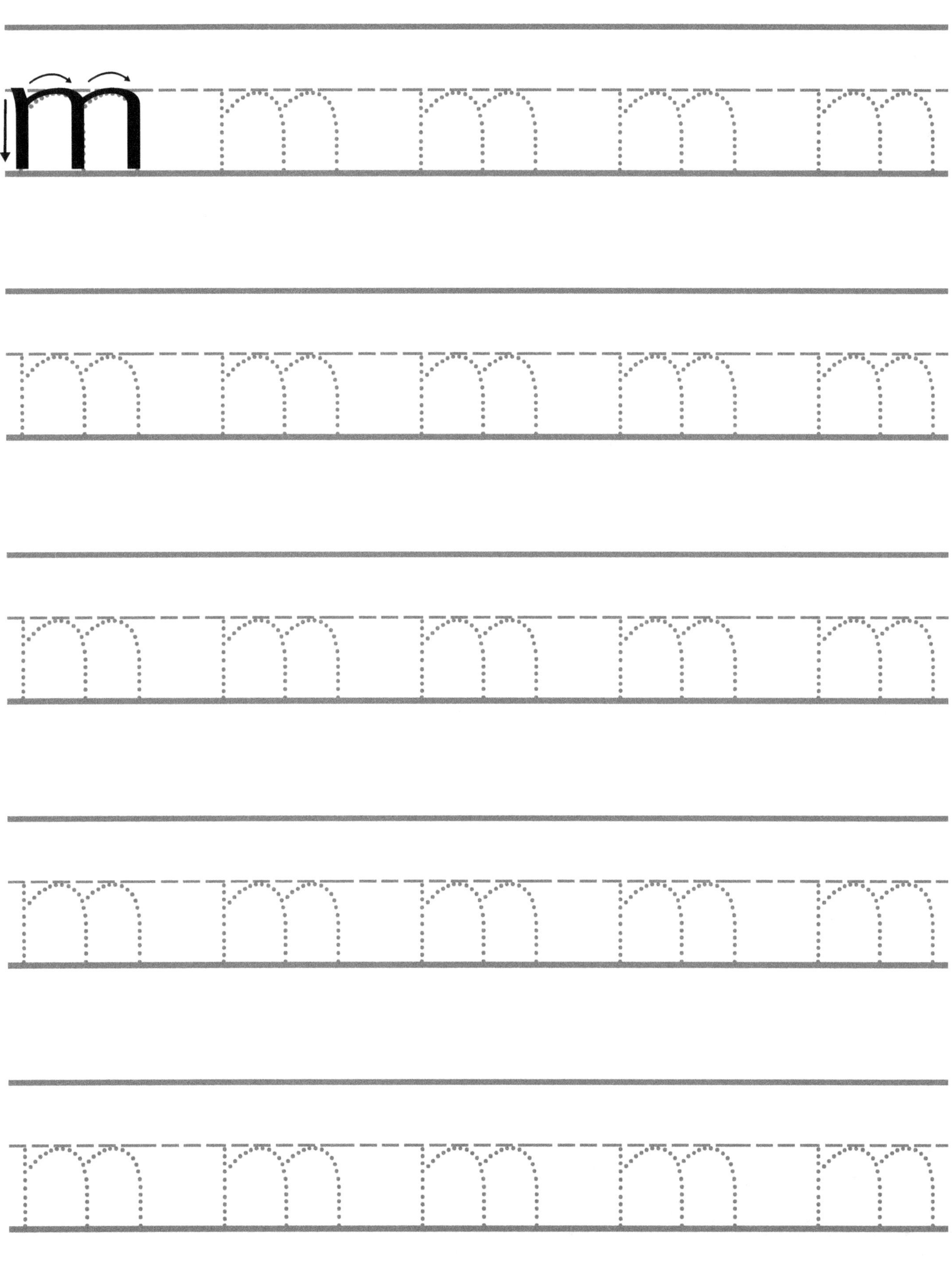

N is for....

Ninja

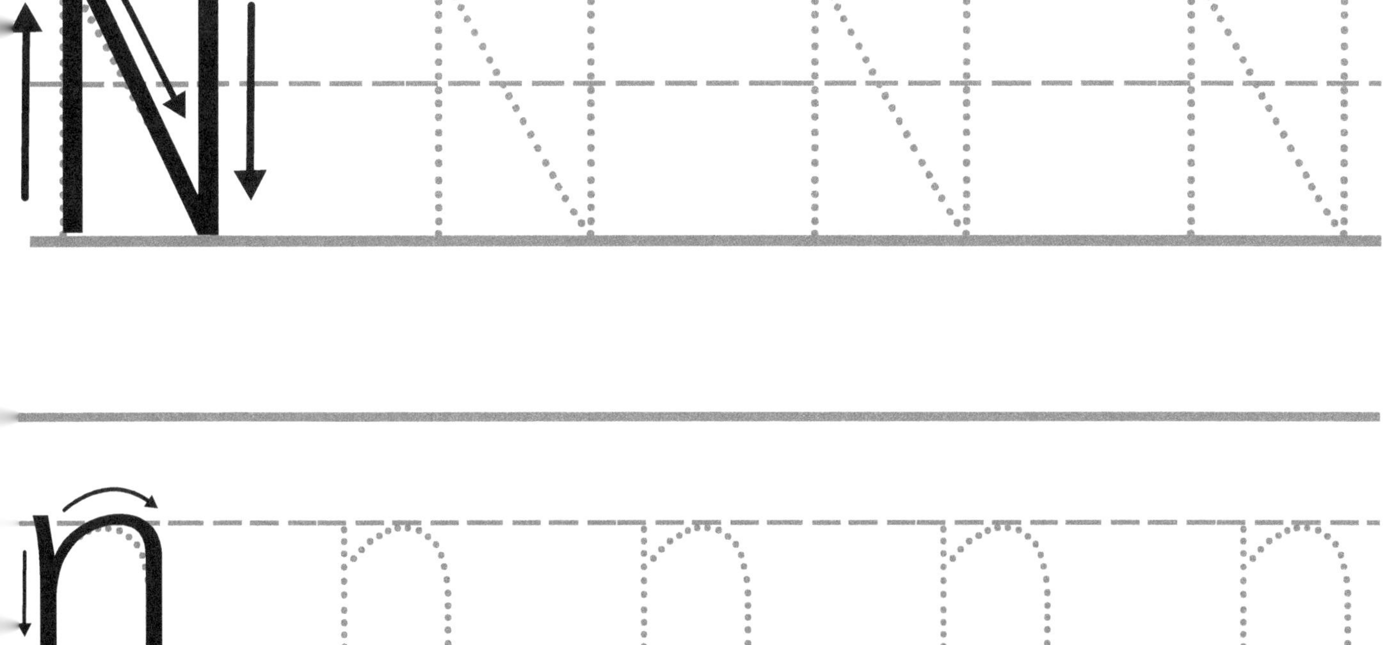

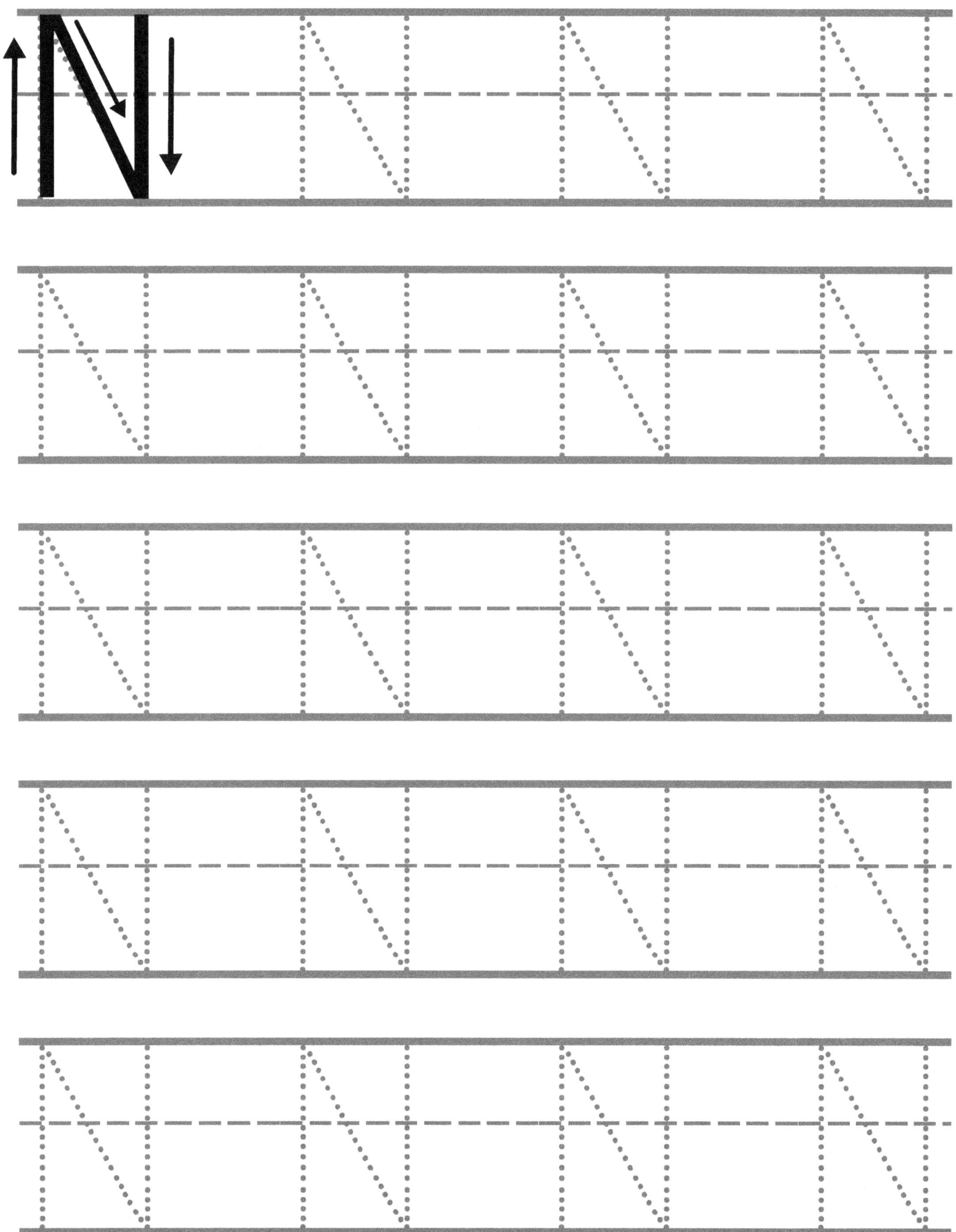

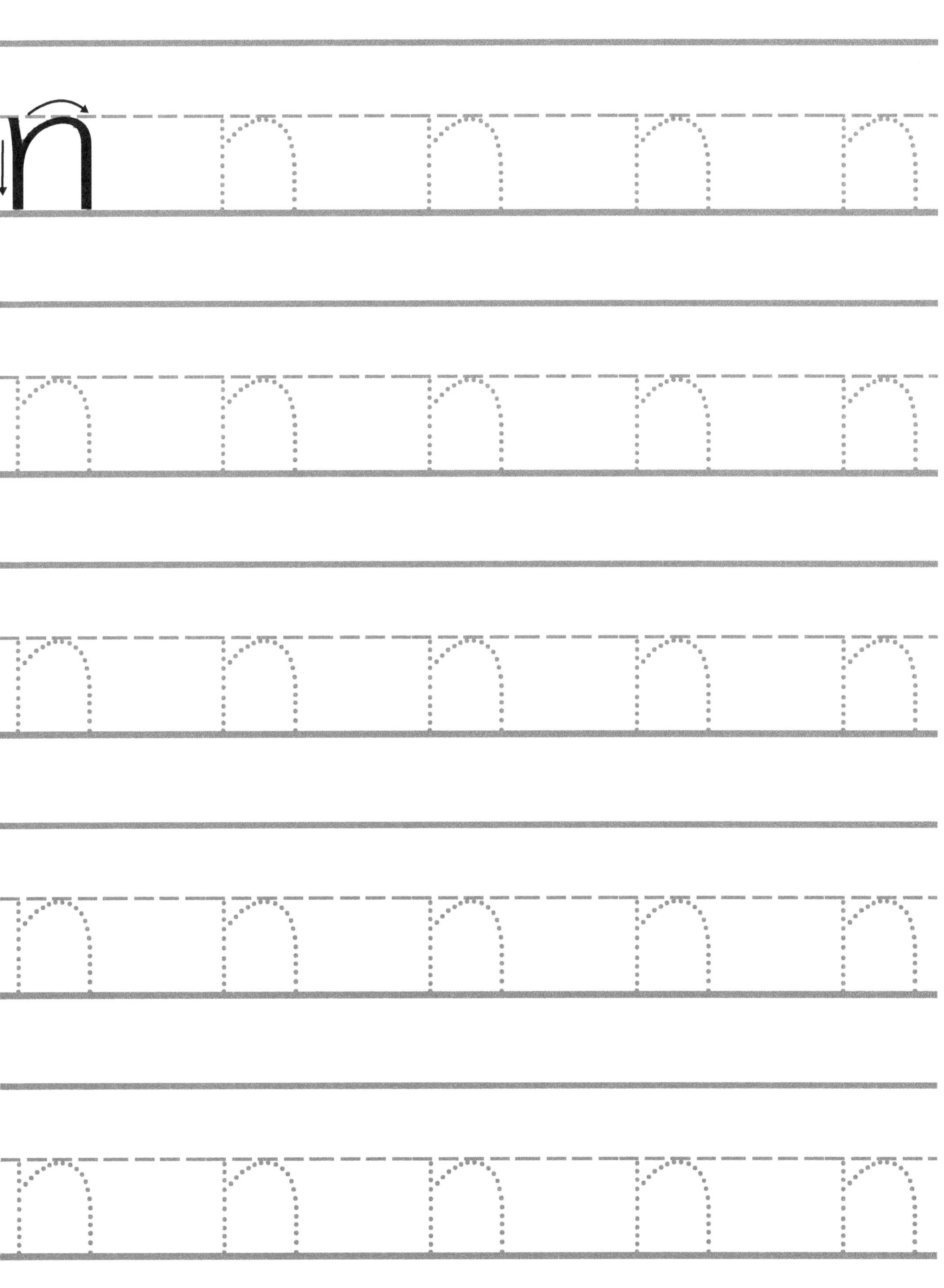

O is for....

Owl

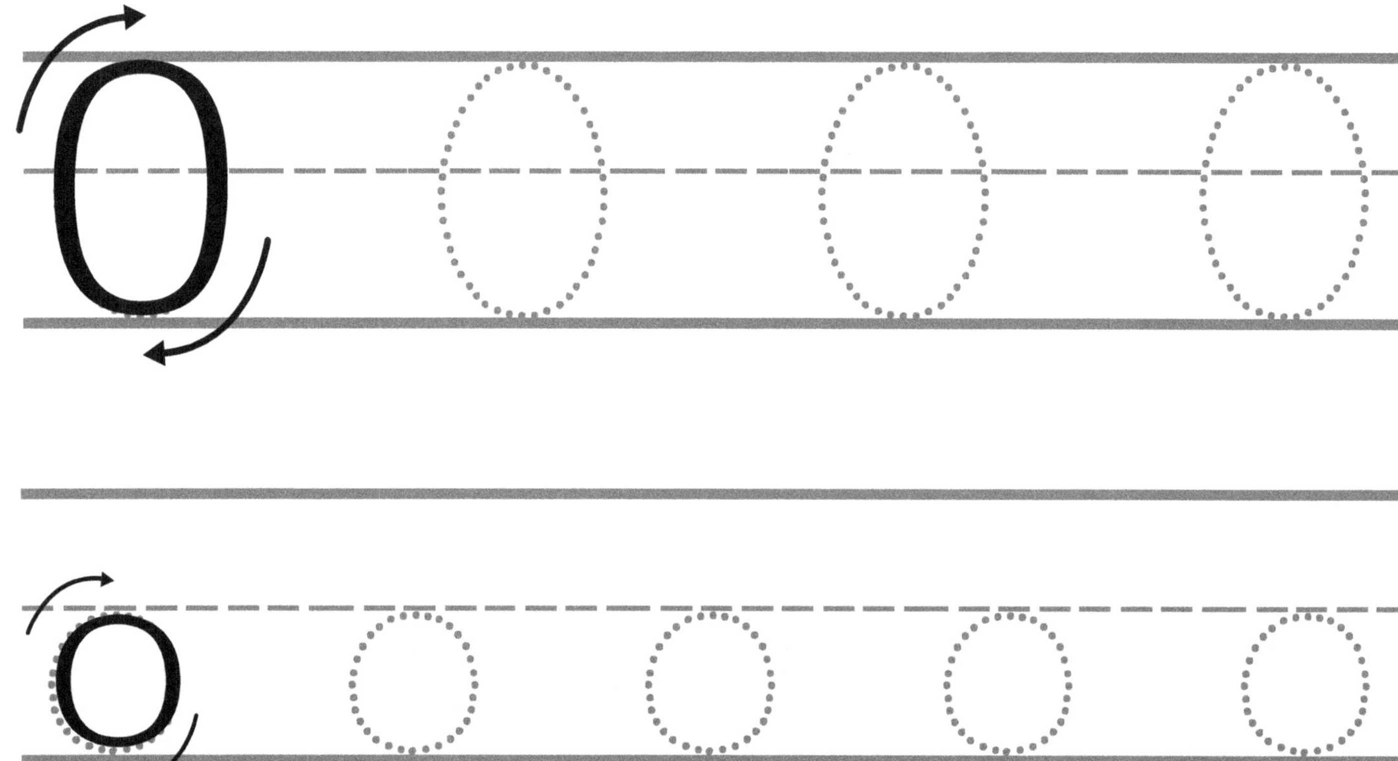

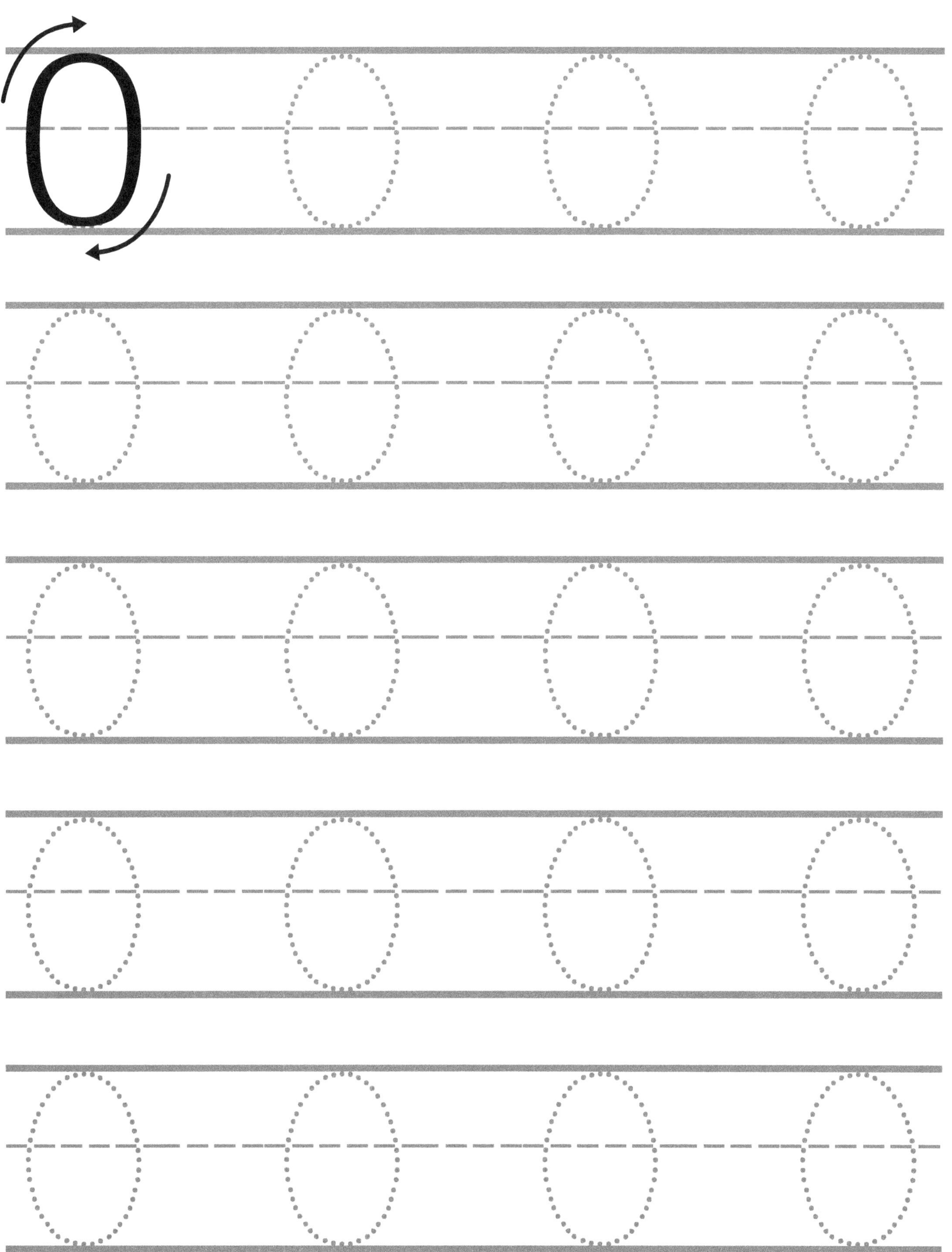

O

P is for....

Panda

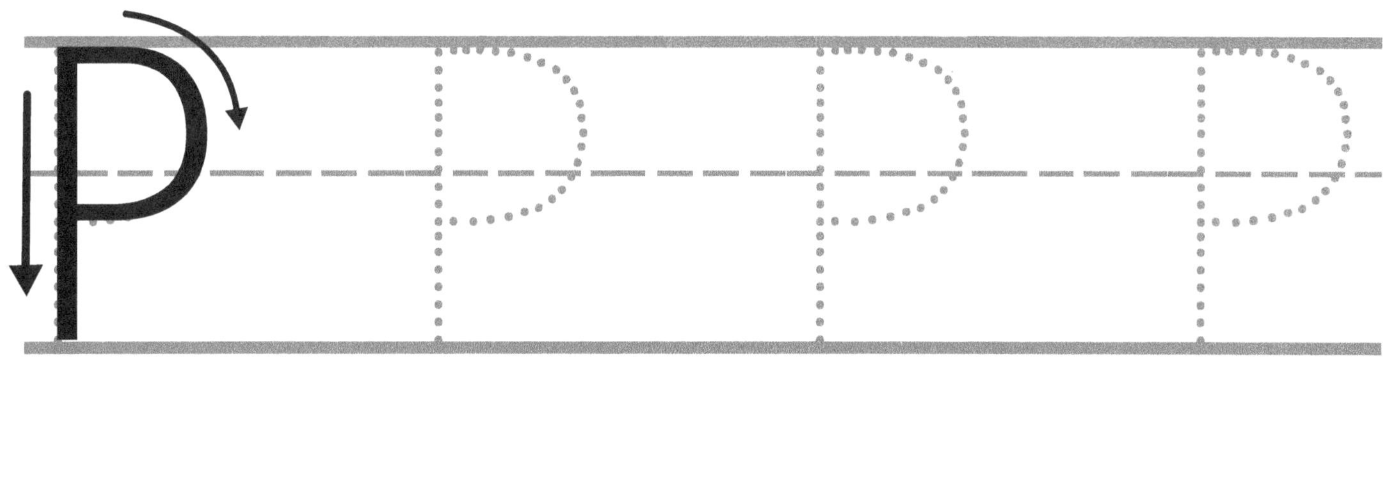

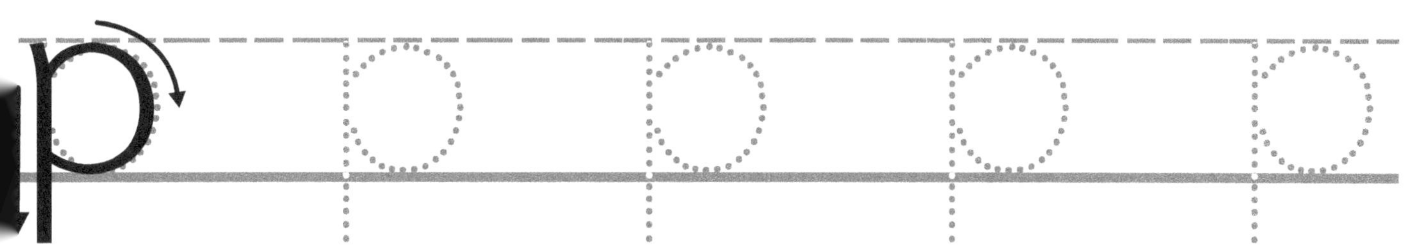

p

Q is for....

Quill

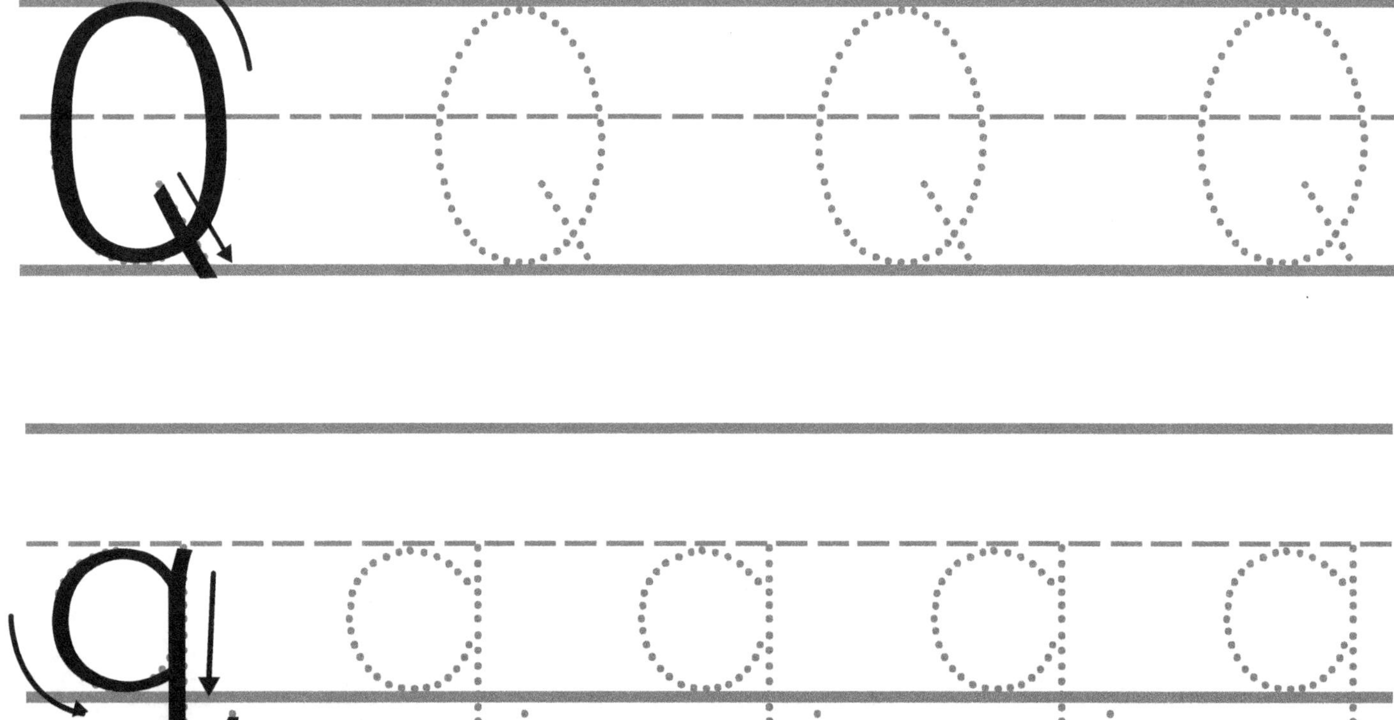

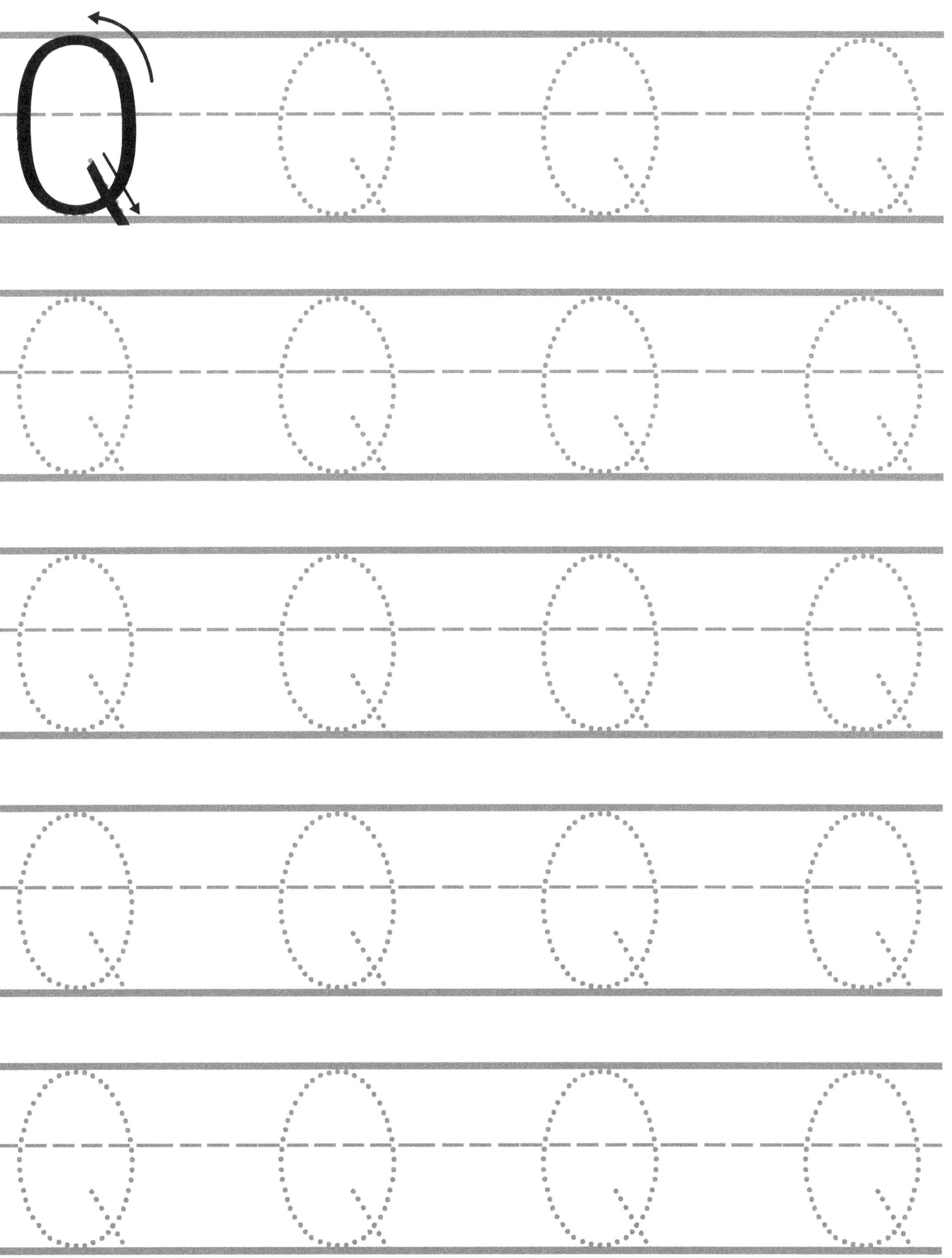

a

R is for....

Robot

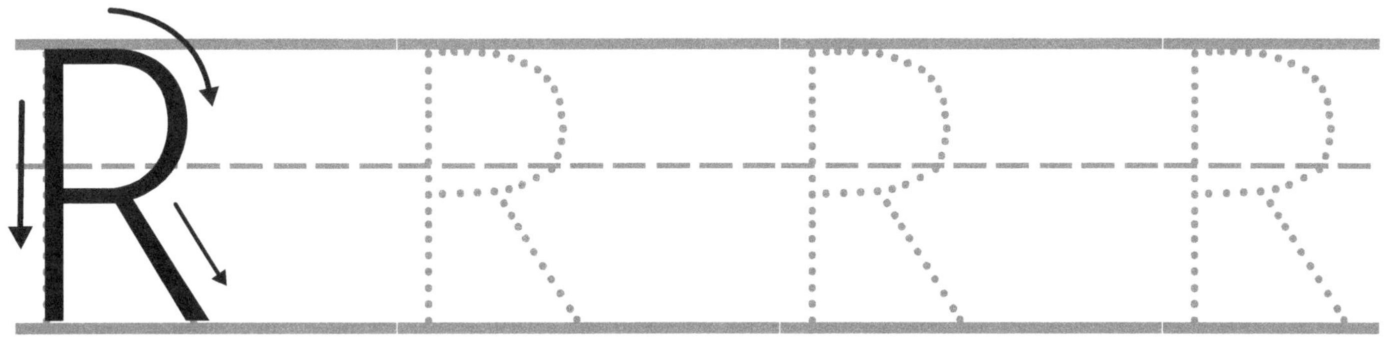

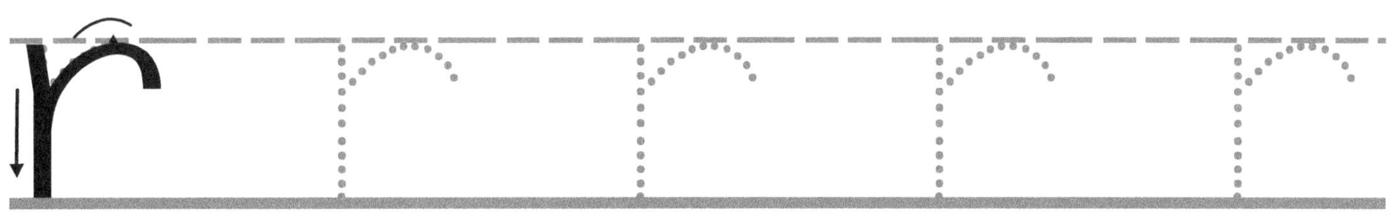

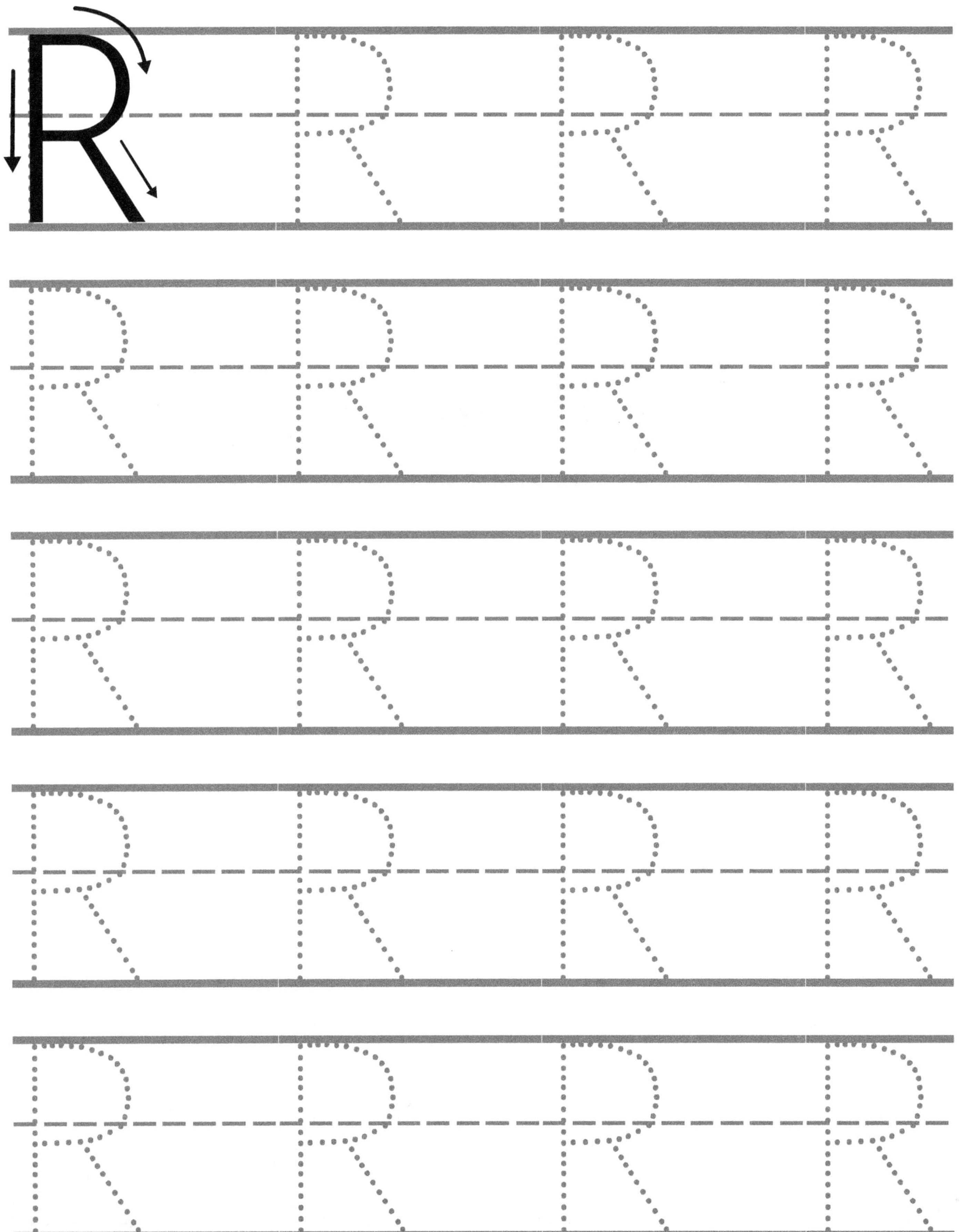

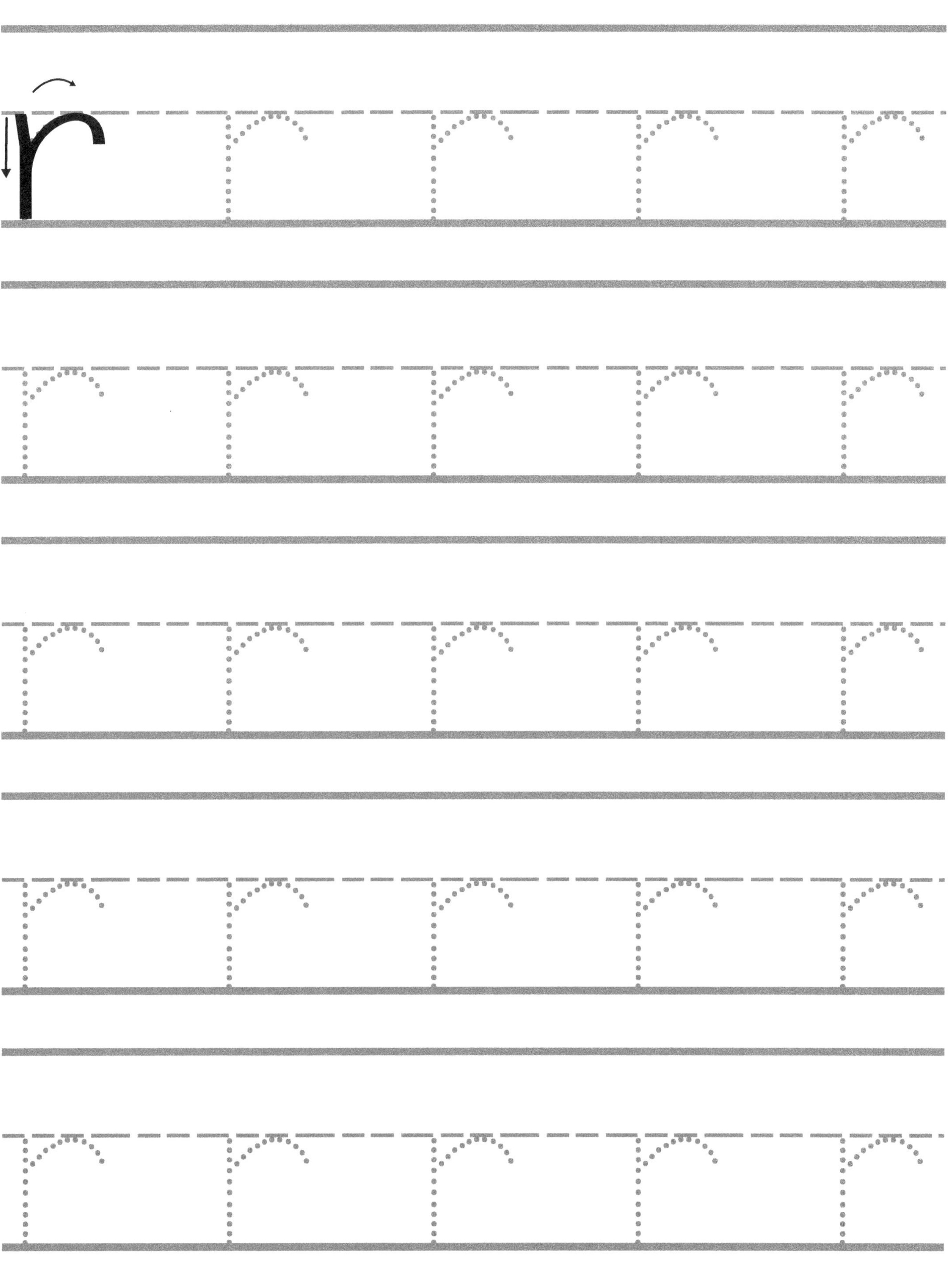

S is for....

Star

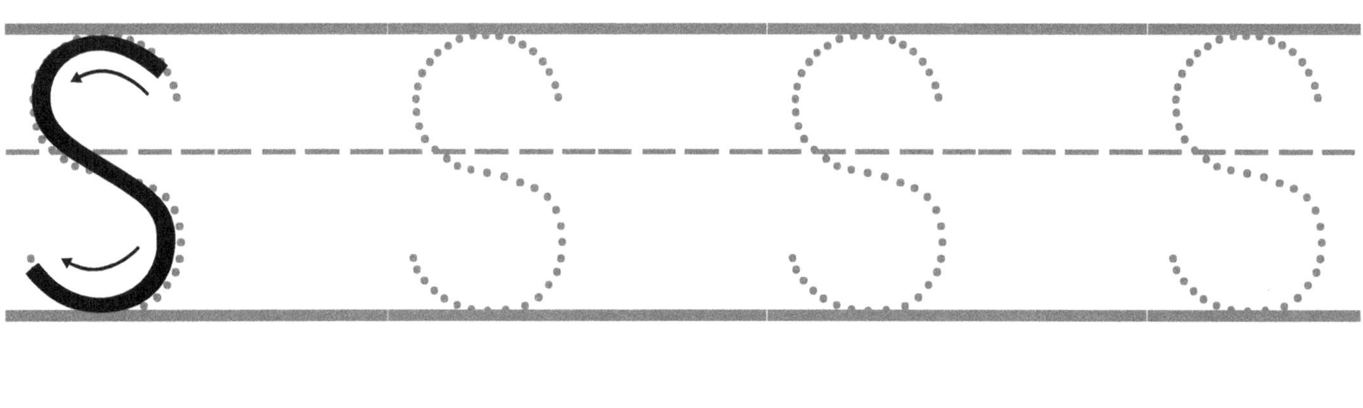

S

S

T is for....

Turtle

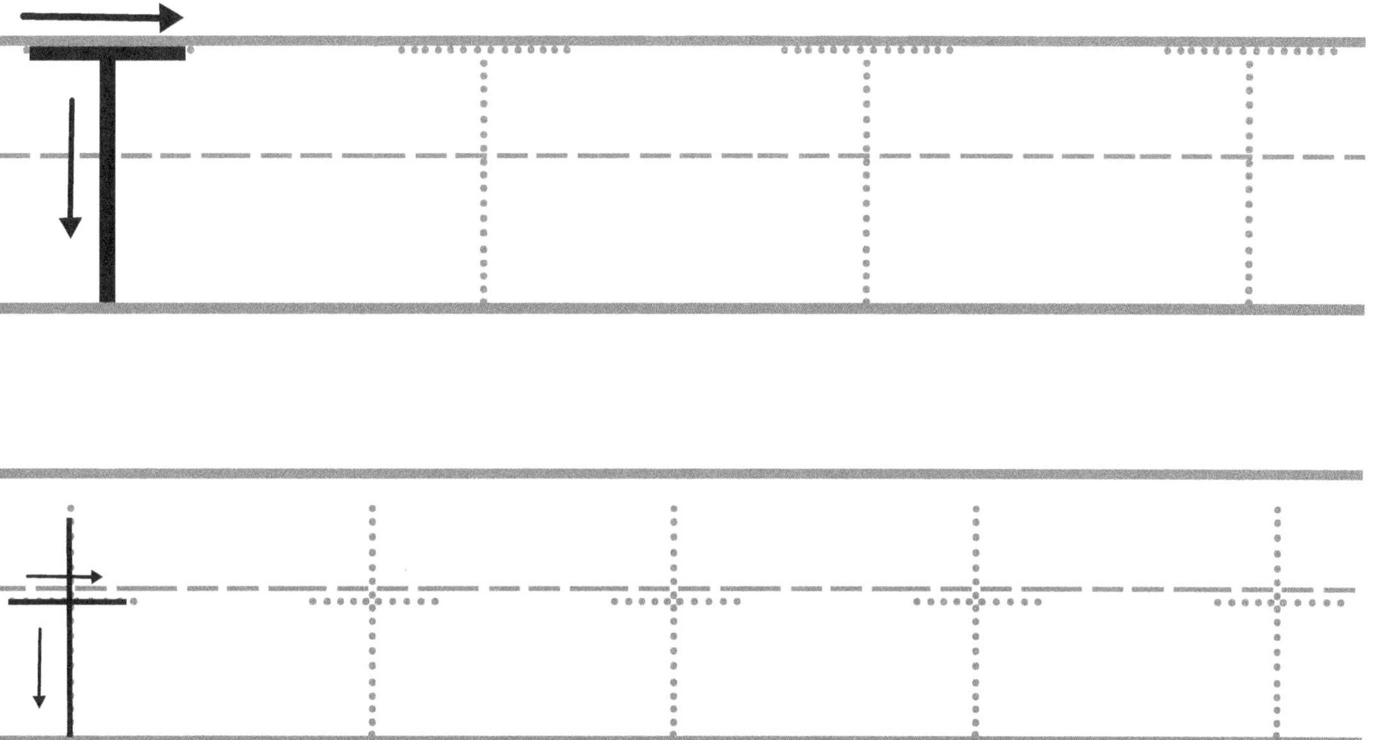

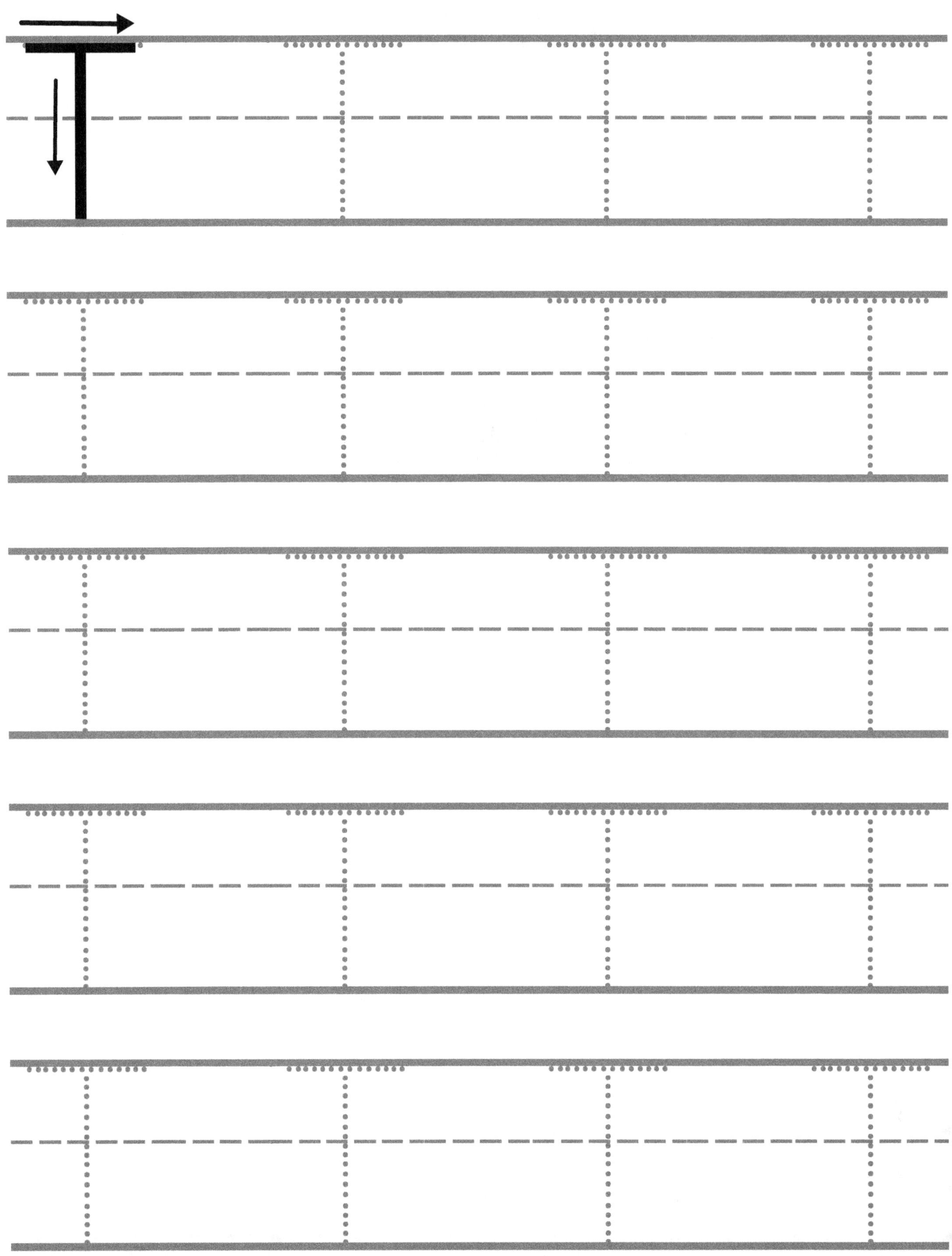

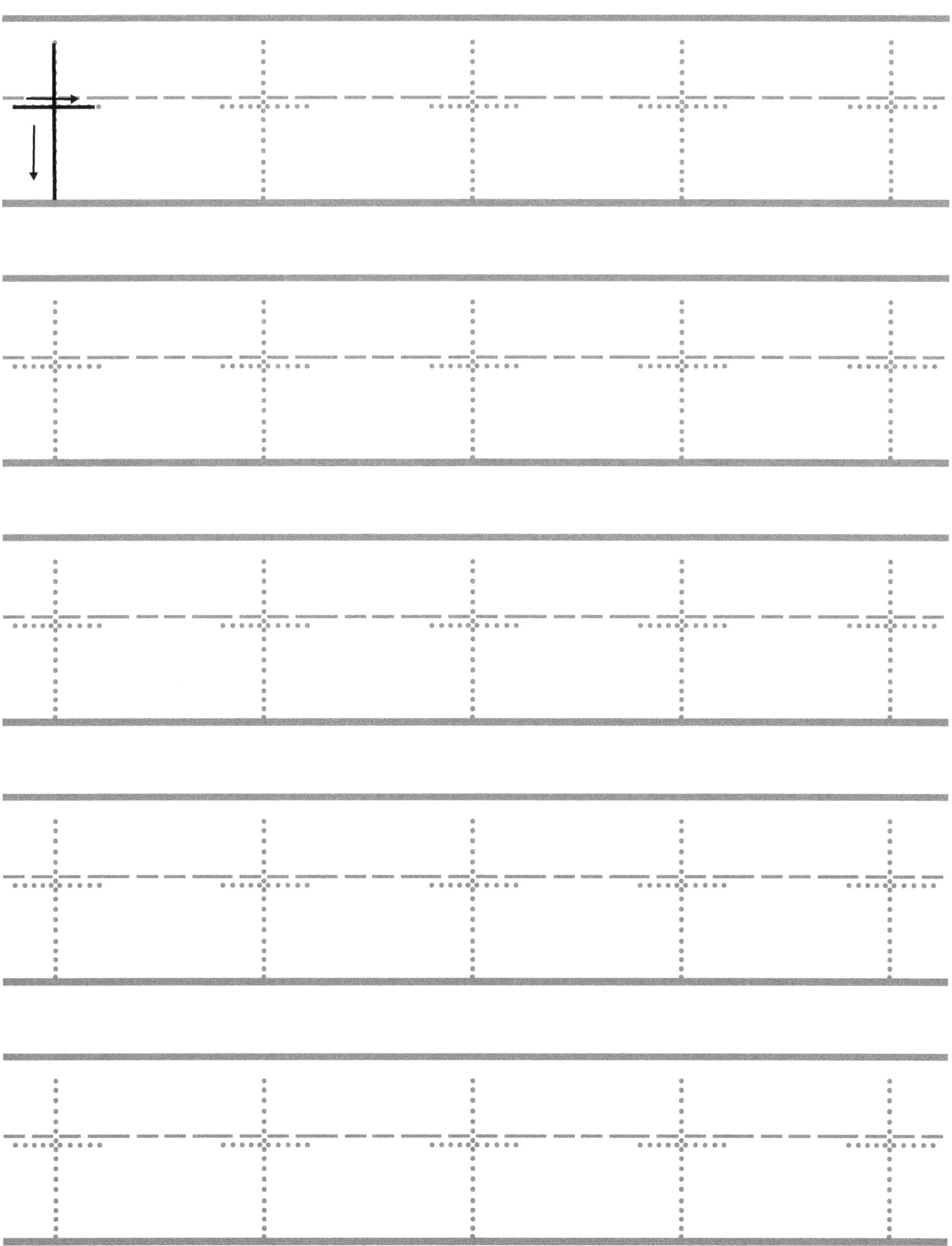

U is for....

Umbrella

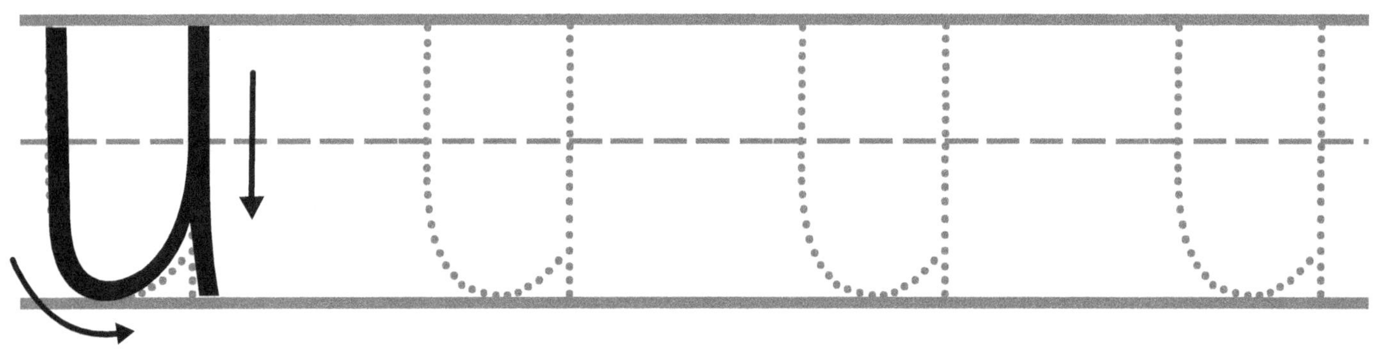

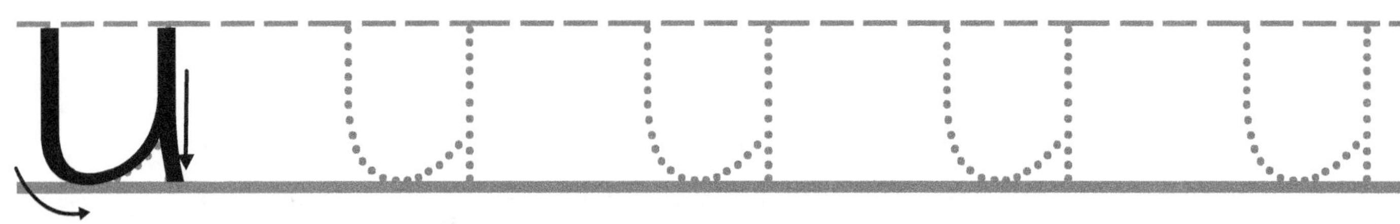

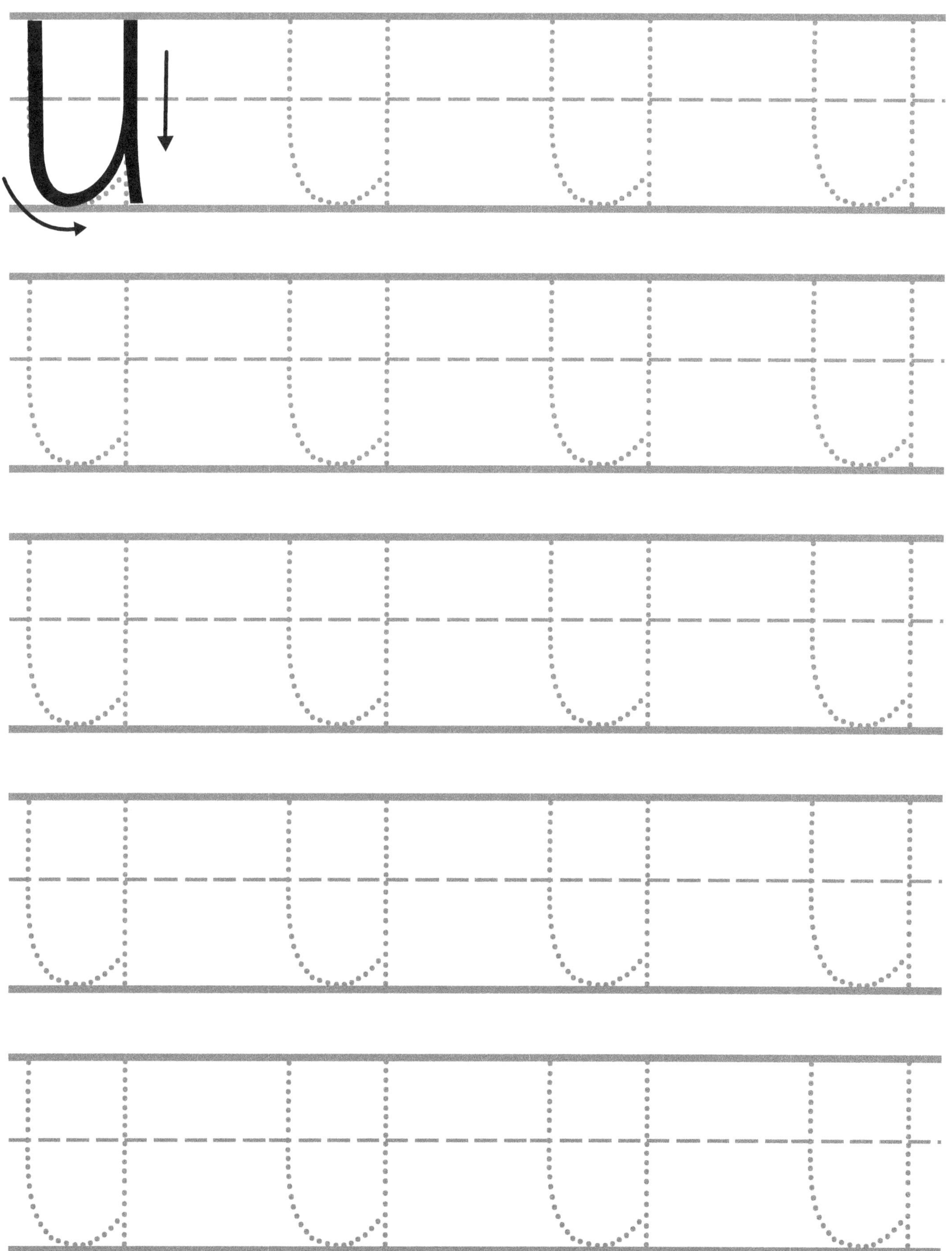

u

V is for....

Vehicle

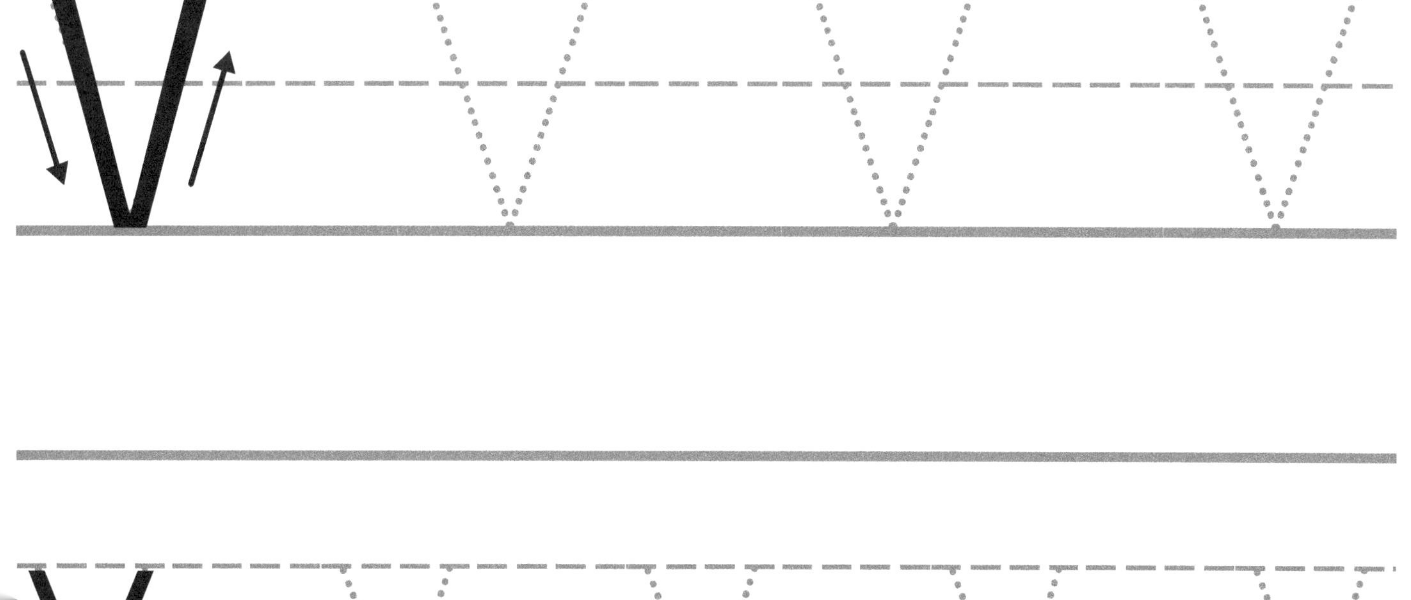

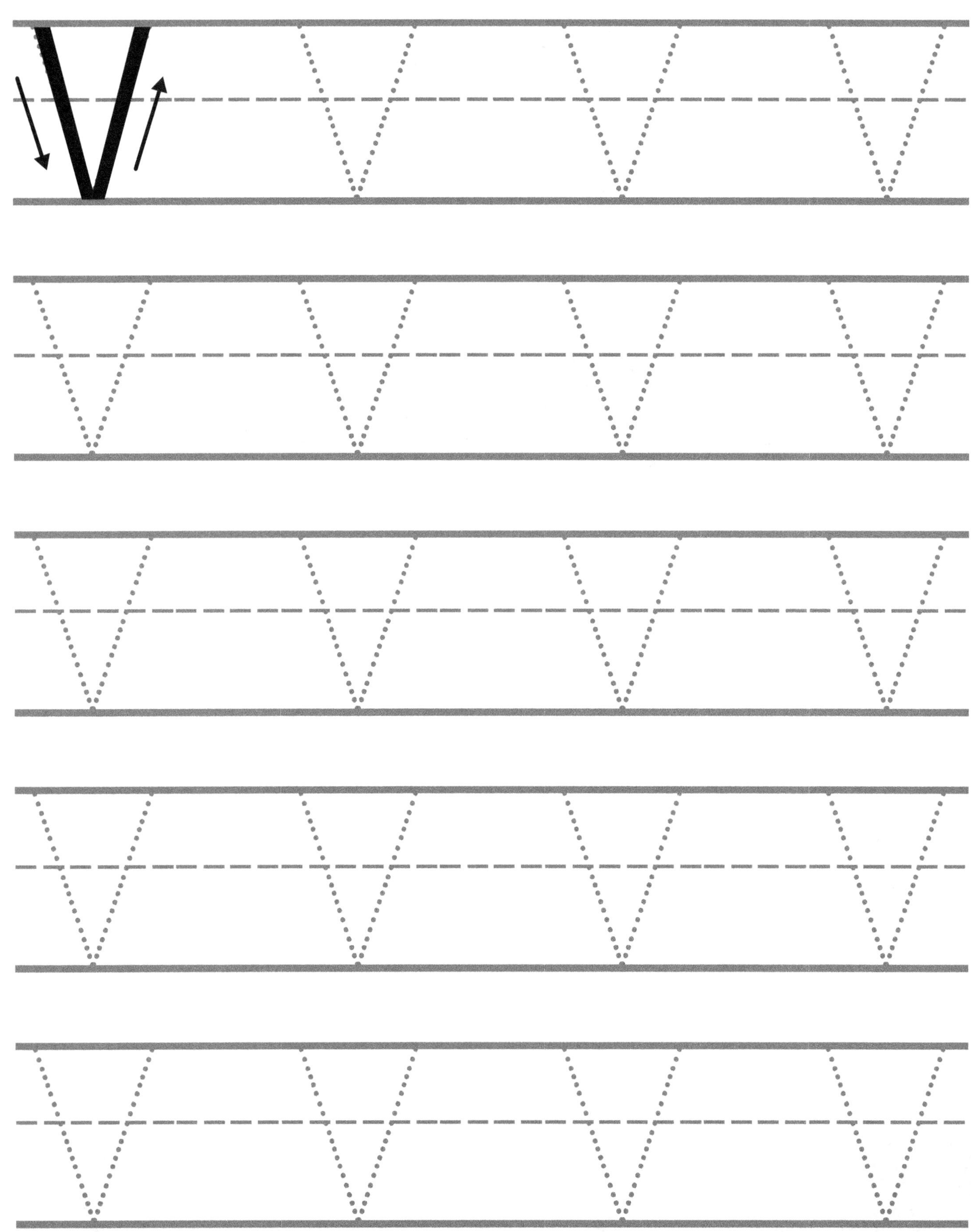

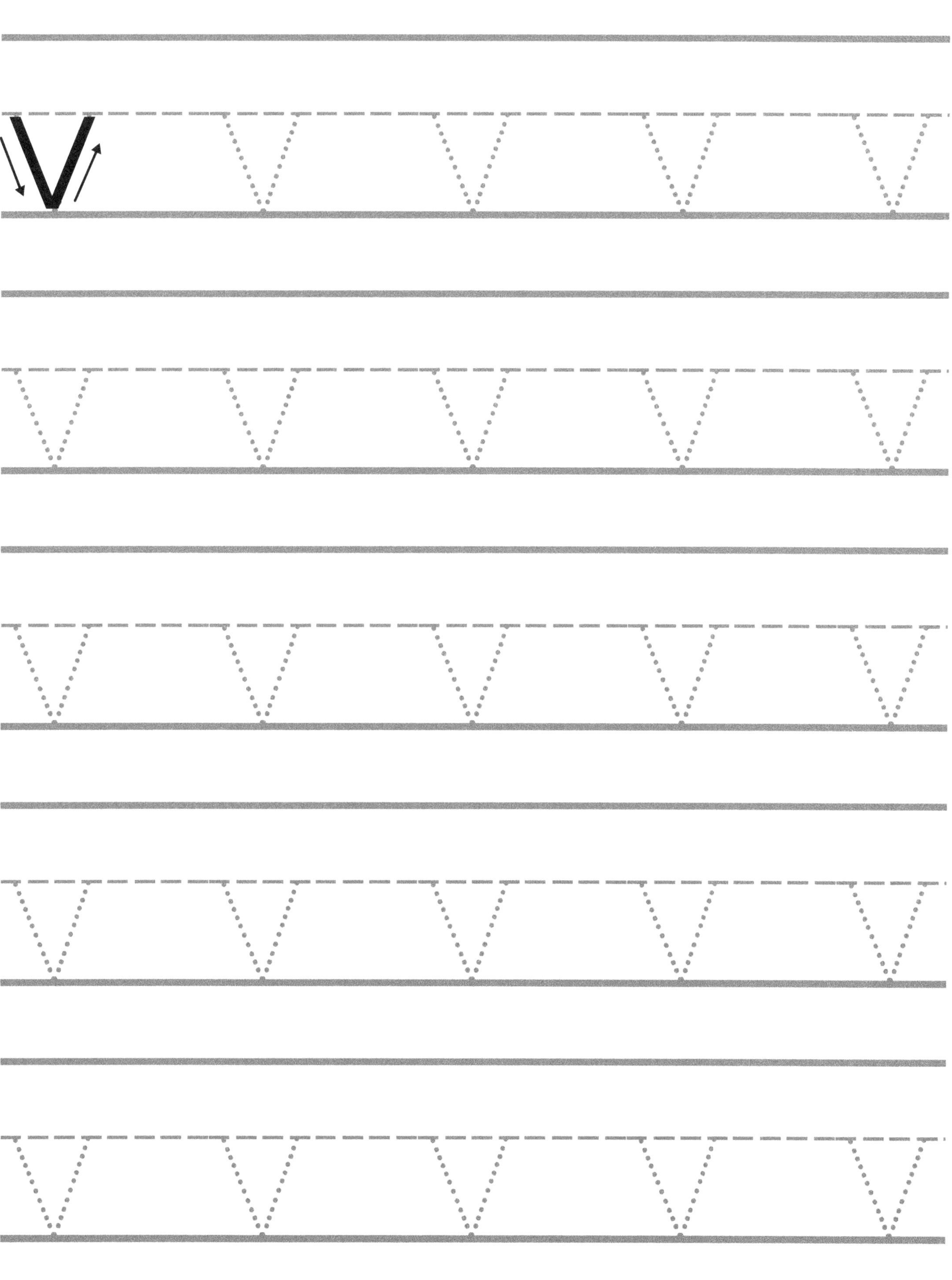

W is for....

Wolf

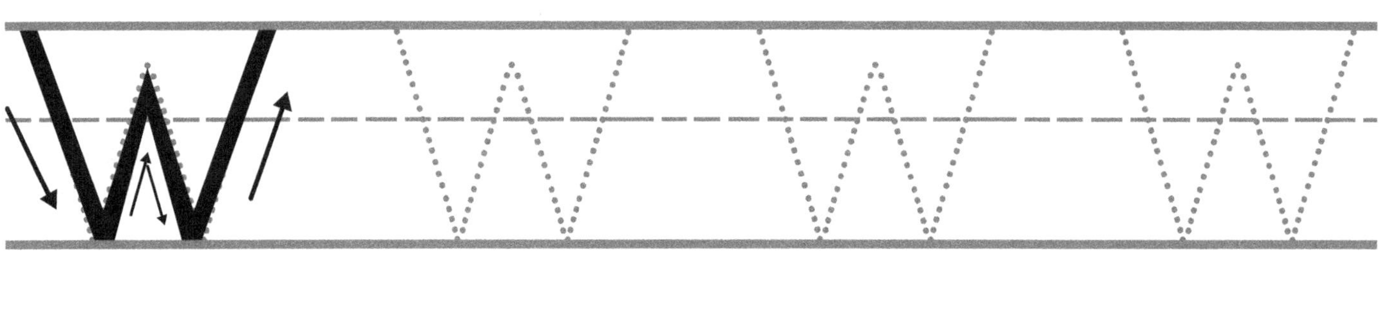

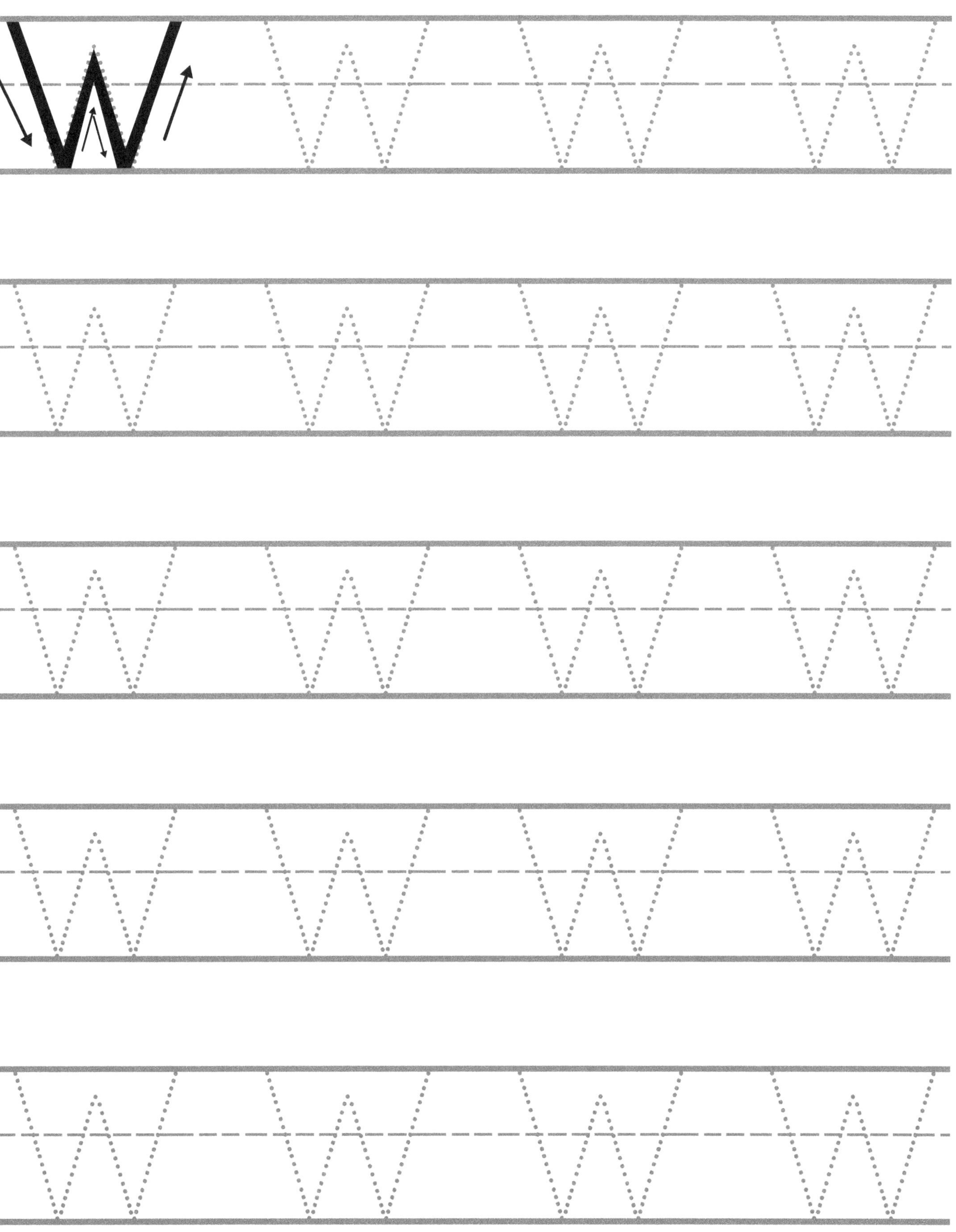

X is for....

X-ray

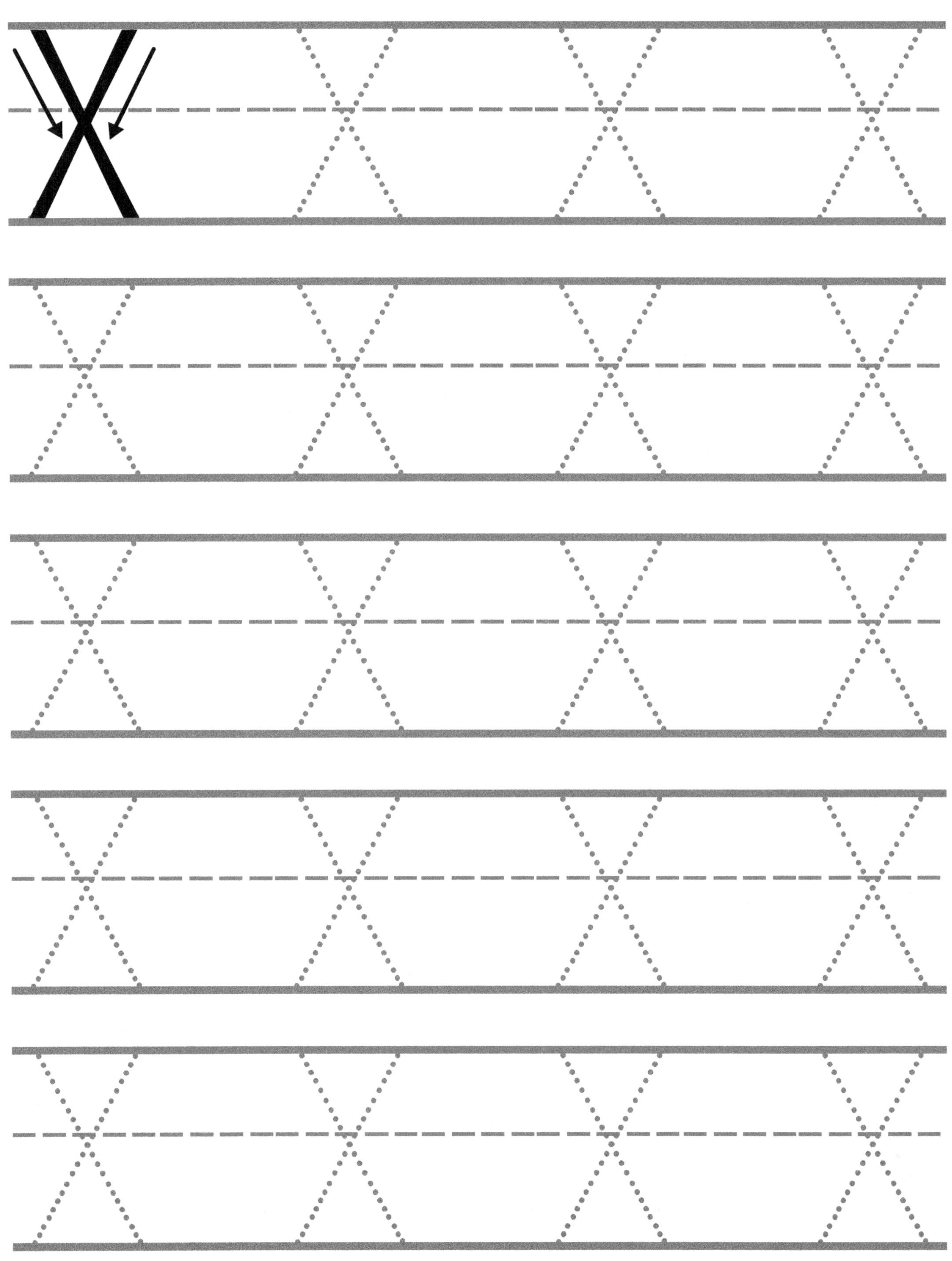

Y is for....

Yo Yo

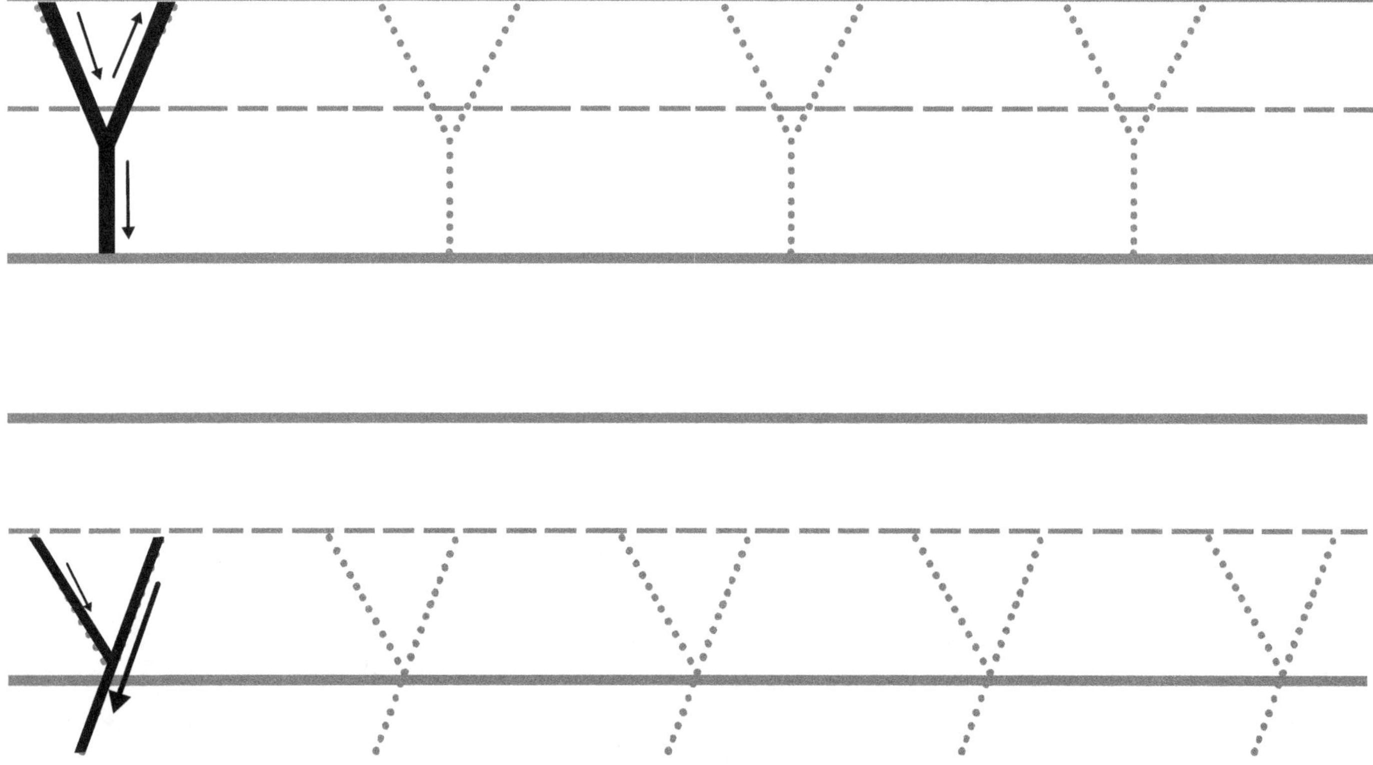

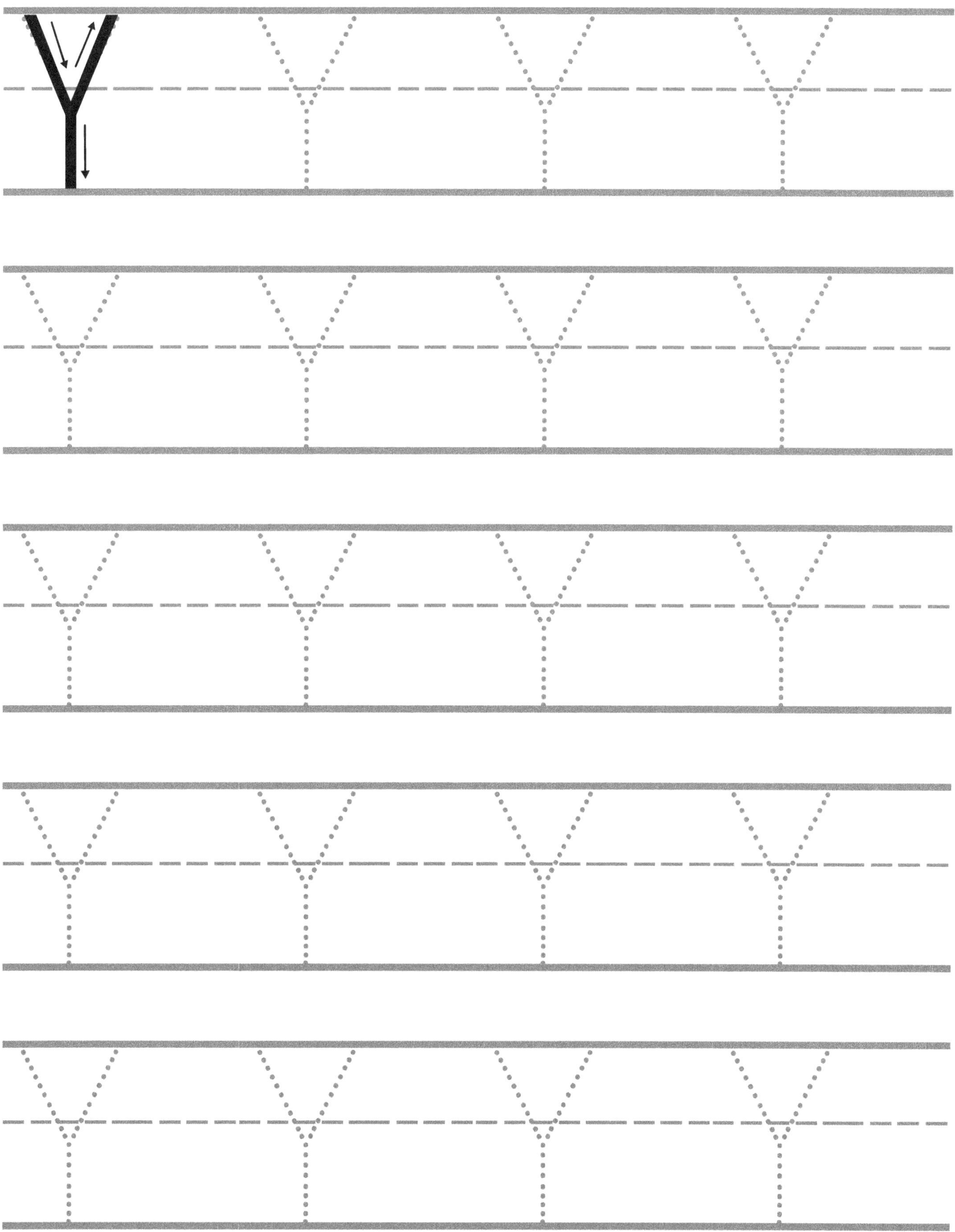

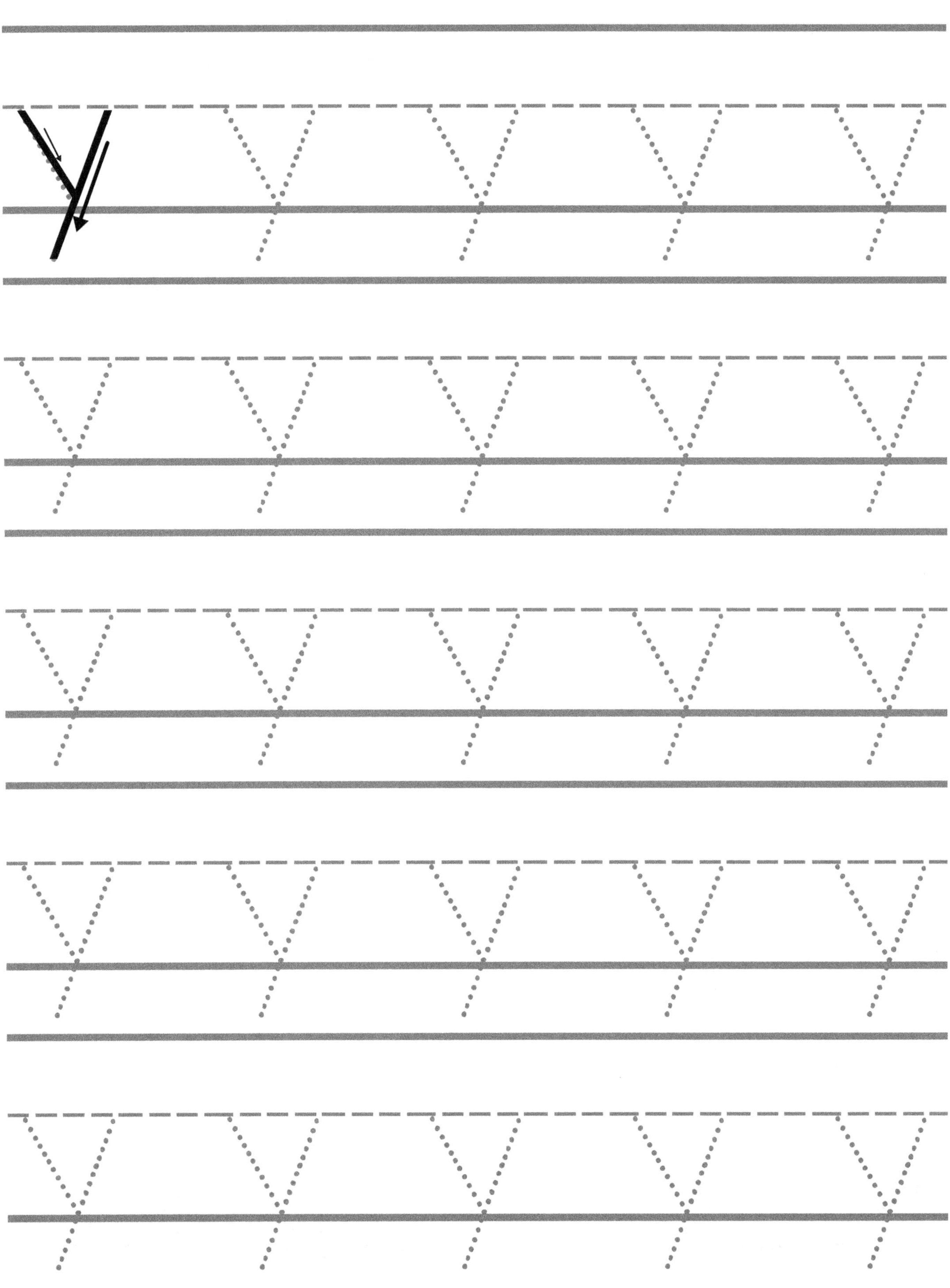

Z is for....

Zebra

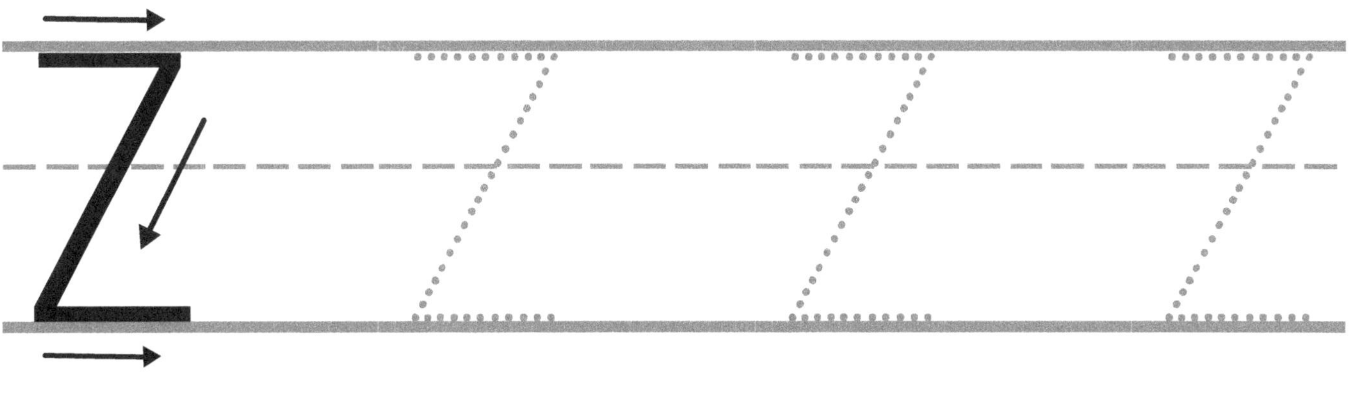

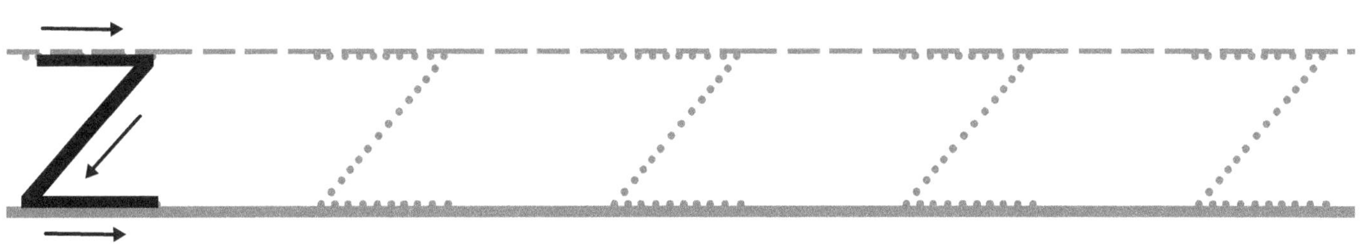

Z